Peace Off
AND BE WHAT YOU ARE

KARL RENZ

Peace Off
AND BE WHAT YOU ARE

KARL RENZ

Edited By
Manjit Achhra

A Division of Maoli Media Private Limited

Peace off!
Because That what you are doesn't need any peace
And that what needs peace will never find peace.
For there's no peace in the world,
there's no peace in anything because they are all ideas!
The peace you are, you never lost.
That what you never lost, you cannot find in any of this so-called ... whatever you call it.
The peace you can experience is not the peace you are...
because the peace you can experience is different from something else.

KARL RENZ

Peace Off: And Be What You Are

Copyright © 2017 Karl Renz

First Edition: January 2017

Published By
ZEN PUBLICATIONS
A Division of Maoli Media Private Limited

60, Juhu Supreme Shopping Centre,
Gulmohar Cross Road No. 9, JVPD Scheme,
Juhu, Mumbai 400 049. India.
Tel: +91 9022208074

eMail: info@zenpublications.com
Website: www.zenpublications.com

Book Design: Red Sky Designs, Mumbai
Cover Image: Detail of a painting by Karl Renz

ISBN 978-93-85902-47-5

All rights reserved. No part of this book may be reproduced or transmitted in any form or by any means, electronic or mechanical, including photocopying, recording, or by any information storage and retrieval system without written permission from the author or his agents, except for the inclusion of brief quotations in a review.

Contents

Peace Off! And Be The Peace You Are — 11

Be The Freedom That's Free From The Idea Of Freedom. — 47

The Peace You Experience Is Not The Peace You Are — 82

What You Gain, You Lose Again — 117

The Intellect Is An Infinite Grave Of Dead Concepts — 152

That What You Are Doesn't Need Any Peace, And That What Needs Peace Will Never Find Peace — 187

Other Books by Karl Renz

- Undecided: *Neti-Neti*
- Commentaries On The Gospel Of Thomas
  Excerpts from the Marsanne talks
- A Little Bit Of Nothingness
  81 Observations On The Unnamable
- The Song of Irrelevance
  Meditation of what you are
- Heaven and Hell
- Am I - I Am
- May It Be As It Is
  The Embrace of Helplessness
- Worry and be Happy
  The Audacity of Hopelessness
- Echoes of Slience
  Avadhut Gita Revisited
- If You Wake Up, Don't Take It Personally
  Dialogues in the Presence of Arunachala
- The Myth of Enlightenment
  Seeing Through the Illusion of Separation

ACKNOWLEDGEMENT

The Publishers wish to thank
Anjali Walsh, Hemant Nadkarni and Sanjay Inamdar
for their invaluable help in making this book possible.

∽

Chapter One

Peace Off!
And be the peace you are

Q: You speak about Trinity. But it's only One, the beingness…

K: You can say Reality is realizing itself in trinity. So, trinity is a realization of Reality but not Reality. The Absolute Being is realizing itself as trinity.

Q: When I experience this…

K: When 'I' experiences this, it's already too late. Whatever starts with 'I' is too late! When the doubtful 'I' starts something, doubtful experiences appear. From the doubtful experience of 'I' the doubtful experiences of whatever happens, happens. The false creates the false. The 'I' is already false and out of the false 'I', the falsity continues.

Q: It's just out of curiosity, not a real question…

K: That's the curious guy. The false is always curious about what is right. The unreal wants to become the real but it will never become real. It tries very hard to become real but the unreal will always remain unreal. And that what is real never needs to question itself because the real is real anyway. The unreal always has this tendency of making itself real but it will never succeed. You can go home now! [Laughter]

The whole Consciousness is only there because the 'I' is there. Since the 'I' is false, the Consciousness is false. Whatever happens is Consciousness. So there are only false happenings. But you cannot get rid of them because they don't exist. It's amazing!

Q: It's too fast for me...

K: I have this problem, I cannot talk slowly. I'm the antidote of John De Ruiter. [Laughter]

Q: I had an insight that it is not trinity, it is only One...

K: Who says it is not three? Maybe it's four. Maybe it's not even one? Who needs to know that? And who now claims that it cannot be that? You have an insight? 'I saw that there are no three'. Maybe there is a tree but no three. [Laughter]

But when there's no trinity, there's trinity because if there's one who says there's no trinity, there has to be trinity. You confirm that there's trinity, just like an atheist who says there's no God, confirms that there is one. Because the God who is not there, has to be so that he cannot be. It's amazing! The atheists really confirm that there's a God. So, you confirm that there is a trinity by saying there's no trinity. If you say there's no devil, there's a devil. Amazing! If you say there's no 'me', for sure there's a 'me'!

Q [Another visitor]: When I ask who is Ramana, it feels like an open space. But when I ask, 'Who am I?' the attention comes back to the body and it's heavy and unpleasant. The body is disturbed...

K: If the question, 'Who Is Ramana' works better, than just forget the 'Who Am I', it's the same. If Ramana works better for disappearance of ideas, than it's your way. But don't say, 'Who Is Karl?'. Don't go so far! [Laughter]

Just forget the 'I' and ask 'Who Is Ramana'... maybe that works for you. Then you disappear in the cosmic-comic strip of life.

Whatever works! Don't just follow what is being said. Whatever works for you is right for you. Trust your inner guru because he knows best. Whatever brings the resonance is exactly what has to happen. There's no religion for What-you-are. You have to lose your religion and all the religions around you because the only God you can trust is What-you-are. And if God wants to ask 'Who Is Ramana?', then God is right.

Q [Another visitor]: I cannot connect with people...

K: Be happy! [Laughter] Everyone wants to be detached and now she's complaining that she's too much detached. Be happy that you're detached.

Q: My mind says, I must be open, I must love everyone...

K: I think you're not in the right place here [Laughter] maybe you went to wrong teachers before. They have implanted the ideas like 'you have to'. Or maybe in your surroundings they must have said, you must have an open heart. And you always fail and complain, 'Bloody me, why am I so stupid? Why am I so closed? Poor me! Everyone else is open, but me'. Forget these open heart masters. They have the most closed heart – these open heart masters. Whoever claims that he has an open heart, has one heart too many. [Laughter]

This ownership of the heart knot is the only thing that makes you suffer. Having heart is hell! *Being* Heart, not *knowing* heart – that's your natural state. But not *having* a heart, and especially not having an *open* heart! [Laughter] Then walking around and selling your open heart to everyone. Then saying 'Oh, I see you, you're still closed, follow me'. It's like fishermen fishing for rotten fish and then selling it to others. The little fish of an open heart concept.

I had a visitor in Koh Samui and she said, you must have an open heart. Mooji confirmed me, Eckhart Tolle confirmed me. I said, 'I, for sure, not'. [Laughter] Because whatever needs to be confirmed, is false. Finished! Especially when someone like Mooji or Eckhart Tolle confirms you. [Laughter] What an idea! The truth that you can agree to, for sure is not the truth. Fuck it all! [Laughter] You can sell that truth, you can make money with that truth because there are many buyers who want to buy the false because they're living by the false. Everyone who wants to buy something wants to own something, and then he buys that what is false. What to do? It's the biggest business on earth.

Q [Another visitor]: Can you talk about avoiding the void?

K: That's a joke because you *are* the void who wants to avoid the void. That's the joke! You're afraid about That What-you-are. You *are* the void. And what is the nature of the void? The void is the absence of what?

Q: Everything...

K: ...of whatever you can imagine. There's no imagining in the void. In the Absolute void, there's no one who imagines something what can be imagined. It's a total void – absolute absence of any concept of what you are and what you are not. And you're afraid of That what youare, which is the Absolute absence of any presence of What-it-is and What-it-is-not – that's a joke! You are That and you try to avoid that What-you-are. And by avoiding that What-you-are, you suffer! What a joke! It's unexplainable why that happens.

Q: What to do?

K: You will only give up avoidance if you are destroyed by... whatever. It can only be done by What-you-are... but not by the one who wants to avoid something. And trying *not* to avoid is feeding that avoider. Whatever you try now from that position doesn't work. Even trying *not* to avoid, is avoiding the avoidance. So, I sit here and tell you that you have to be in *spite* of the avoider avoiding what can be avoided... which is actually unavoidable. So, I sit here and tell you that you cannot avoid being What-you-are. So, just *be* it! Be That what you cannot *not* be, because that's unavoidable, because it waits for you anyway. This phantom that rises, will disappear again. It came and it will be gone – this avoider. So why not be That in the presence of it or in the absence of it? Why wait for it to be gone? It will be gone one day and you will be the leftover again because the leftover cannot avoid itself. You are that Reality which is unavoidable.

And now you realize yourself as a person, so what? The person came and the person will be gone... hello, goodbye. So why wait for it to disappear to become What-you-are? You will never *become* it because you never lost What-you-are. So, just be that! The phantom collector will collect some stupid ideas on the way. Then it will be proud of his collection of the inside (insight) and the outside, but by *none* of that he can avoid that he will be gone one day, and you *still* will be What-you-are. All the collection of the scriptures, all the insights, all truth and all ideas came with this body and will go with this body; and you still will be What-you-are – naked as you are. You cannot avoid to be That what you *were* before, what you *are* now and what you *will* be. So why not be *it* now? That which has nothing to gain or to lose here! Come on!

So, what to do? There's nothing to do but just being that what is unavoidable because you cannot avoid to exist as that What-you-are. And as you are That, you realize yourself as whatever. But waiting for someone like the Eagle of consciousness to go to become What-you-are, you may wait forever. The eagle will always be there, like consciousness always trying to know the consciousness. Mind will always mind the mind. So, you better don't wait for it to end because maybe it is as infinite as you are. Imagine! Trinity or not... [Laughter] Waiting for Godot. Waiting for God to come, but God is already here.

But I can just blah, blah, blah about it. I cannot make you What-you-are. I can neither make you, nor unmake you. I cannot give anything, I cannot take anything away from you. So what? I can only point to That but you have to *be* it. And not be in love with the imaginary 'I'. You have to put all your love, all your attention to That what never needs attention. This paradox you cannot solve. Because the Existence you are never needs any attention to exist and that existence that *needs* attention to exist, is false. That's all!

Q [Another visitor]: The other day you said you love not to need any love...

K: You have to drop the relative love so that the love remains.

Q: The next day you said that we cannot let go of our ego because we love it too much...

K: Yes!

Q: So, what to do apart from sitting here?

K: You have to try, but you will fail. As I said before, Buddha failed. And in absolutely failing to know yourself, you are That what you cannot not be because you failed in every way. You even failed in failing. Then you are left as That what you are – the Absolute leftover – like a substratum that substrates everything, even that one who substrates everything. You abstract even the abstractor or you renounce the renouncer as Ramana said. Just renounce the renouncer and be What you are because What-you-are cannot be renounced. And the renouncer renouncing something is a false renouncer renouncing the false world. So, what is the gain of renouncing the world if there's still one left who renounces something? Only the false needs to renounce something. So, renounce the renouncer and be what you are. But how to do that is the question? How to know yourself?

Then the scriptures tell you that you have to know yourself as you know yourself in deep-deep sleep – in the total absence of any presence of one who is or is not. There is a doubtlessness of What-you-are. There is no doubter and nothing that can be doubted in the absolute absence of any presence of living life or any concept ...and still you are. So, every morning this wakes up and then you fall in love again. You cannot stop it. This loving-caring about whatever it is, is your nature. What can you do? You fall in love immediately at first sight every morning and then it starts again.

This helplessness I'm pointing at. You cannot *not* fall in love. Trying *not* to fall in love is already too late because there's already a lover who tries not to be in love. It's too late. And for What-you-are, it's always too early because there's no one who needs anything. But the moment you wake up, there's one awake and then the lover is there and the lover loves and cares about what is. So, what to do?

Every intention is an intention of love; good intention everywhere! What to do? And you cannot leave what you are because you are That what is realizing itself and you cannot be more or less as you are. This is What-you-are. You *are* That – so *be* it! There's no way out of it. And when you *are* That, there's no imprisonment. There's not even an idea of *moksha* or freedom or anything because you *are* That.

But now when you imagine that you are an inmate, that you are imprisoned in something, you confirm that 'you' need something. The only way out is to know yourself as That. But there's no 'knower' in it. This is the kingdom of What-you-are; the kingdom of Heart and not the kingdom of a King. You want to be the King of this kingdom, the ruler of this universe. That will never happen! The Heart cannot be ruled by anything. And the kingdom of Heart is without a king. The king that appears in the morning... you must be jo-king! He can never be the king of Heart.

Buddha failed to rule his kingdom because he tried to end suffering, he tried to get enlightened. But he failed. He could not end the suffering of the world, he could not end whatever. So, he failed in every sense. From the absolute failing comes... No way out! Whatever you do is futile. You cannot change your realization. As Reality you don't need to and that what is part of the realization has no power at all. The Absolute Dreamer doesn't *need* to change the dream and that what is in the dream has no energy to change the dream. So, there's Absolute failing. What to do?

Shanti! Shanti! Shanti!

Q [Another visitor]: You spoke about the deep sleep state...

K: The deep-deep sleep state. There's a difference between deep sleep and deep-deep sleep state. The deep-deep sleep state is the Nature of the deep sleep state. Now there's a presence and the presence of the presence is the Heart of this presence. So, the sleep of the sleep, the nature of deep-sleep, is the deep-deep sleep. That's the Knowledge of deep-deep sleep. The knowledge of this moment is the presence of this presence.

Q: Can you talk about the fourth state of *turiya*?

K: I can talk about it! I rarely find something that I cannot talk about. [Laughter]

Turiya state would be your Natural state where you don't know What-you-are and What-you-are-not anymore. There's no knower who knows what he is and what he is not. There's an absence of one who knows or doesn't know what one is... that's *turiya*. That's your natural state, that's *samadhi*.

Q: What is the difference with the deep-deep sleep state?

K: That is *turiya*. That is the pointer of the *samadhi* of the deep-deep sleep state because there's no one. There's no knower who knows what he is and what he is not. That's *turiya*, your natural state.

Q: In this state whether the eyes are open or closed?

K: There's no body. Who is there in deep-deep sleep?

Q: You are defining *turiya* as the *samadhi* of *sushupti*...

K: ...as Ramana did. The deep-deep sleep *samadhi* is the presence of the presence. That's the fourth state. The three other states are the 'I' or the Awareness state, the 'I Amness' state and 'I am the body' state. But that what is the Heart of it, is *turiya*. That's the heart of deep sleep. The Heart of the father, the Heart of the spirit and the Heart of the son.

Q: Is there one awake or asleep?

K: There's no one – that's the whole problem.

Q: That entity...

K: There's no entity in it. That entit-tea that brings chai, cannot be there because That what is Heart is too shy to have an entity. [Laughter]

Q: So, is it a body location?

K: The body is just a fleeting shadow. But that what is the light is with and without the shadow – come on! There is no entity in Light.

Q: But it is walking around, eating and sitting...

K: ...and shitting... it's a shit factory you know that. And the brain is part of the shit factory because whatever you feed the brain, produces shit.

Q: When Buddha woke up from the *bodhi* tree...

K: He failed, he failed to control his daemons. So, he had to allow them to appear. He failed to control his darkness. He failed in all senses and by that he became that what is light – the *turiya*.

Q: After that...

K: There is no 'after'.

Q: Then he stood up from the tree...

K: There is no *after* that. That's an imaginary Buddhist position. Buddha never went anywhere. He disappeared as what he believed to be and remained as That what he is!

Q: He got the teaching in the fourth state but then he came back...

K: No one comes back from there because no one can be there.

Q: Then who preached at Sarnath and Bodhgaya?

K: Three hundred years later there was a Buddhist convention. Buddha never said any word after that.

Q: No, that's not true... [Laughter]

K: Buddha said there was never any Buddha that walked the earth. Buddha never said a word and that guy who...

Q: Whatever he said was *after* that....

K: You are just a historical mind.

Q: That's false as well...

K: It's *all* false. From a story two thousand and five hundred years ago, you want to use it now as your clever mind. You need a guy from two thousand five hundred years ago to make your point?

Q: I think that's not the point...

K: No, that is the point! You talk from yourself and not from a Buddha two thousand five hundred years ago who *may* have lived or not. It's a maybe.

Q: The point I was trying to make was...

K: Don't use some help from someone else. [Laughter] Tell me something that comes from you.

Q: The *shruti*...

K: Shut up! Tell me something that comes direct from you and not from scriptures or Buddha or a *guru* that you met before. Tell me what is your opinion – only you. What is your original knowledge?

Q: From the little of what I can experience of the what-is state, it seems to me that it is not as blank as what you painted it. On the other side of the void there is a fullness...

K: It's 'foolness'. The foolness is fooling you.

Q: But then so is the void...

K: The void is just a pointer and it's not a fullness or foolness.

Q: A pointer to what?

K: No one knows but that is what you are.

Q: Who comes back to say this?

K: No one comes back.

Q: Who is speaking now?

K: I always say, I have no idea. You are speaking out of scriptures and I have no idea.

Q: What I'm speaking, I also have no idea... [Laughter]

K: No ideas talking. [Laughter] That's what I'm pointing out. Here now, there is Consciousness talking, Consciousness listening and nothing happens.

Q: You said you wanted a trigger, I'm just trying to make you happy... [Laughter]

K: If one pulls the trigger, one should be ready to be shot. [Laughter] But you know, you are like a duck which I can shoot forever and the duck will not die. [Laughter]

Q: Because it's a phantom duck?

K: Yeah. It's like in a fair you have shooting games in which ducks come up. You shoot all the ducks and they pop up again. I have fun shooting but I don't expect the duck to be dead. I shoot the duck that will come back again anyway. [Laughter] Where would be the fun if the duck would really be shot? [Laughter] It's absolutely fair.

Since the beginning, Consciousness talks and shoots all the imaginary ducks and nothing happens. You went to Papaji. He would say, 'Nothing ever happened'. Everyone repeats that but this seed of 'Nothing ever happens' never reaches the soil because it doesn't need to reach.

Q: I think there may be a different way of approaching the question. May be we are overlooking something... [Laughter]

K: The tenth man story again.

Q: [Laughing] What can I do?

K: You are What-you-are when you fail permanently not temporarily.

Q: It's not my fault, is it?

K: But every night you fail temporarily.

Q: Why do you keep using this deep sleep model?

K: Because it's a famous one.

Q: Shankara mentioned it but it is not complete...

K: Shankara wanted to win against Buddhism, that's not my case. He was trying to defeat Buddhism but I'm not interested.

Q: I thought he was trying to explain it...

K: Explaining something what is unexplainable, it's fantastic. He found a concept which maybe you cannot touch. But what is that concept?

Q: I don't know, can you tell me?

K: I'm not interested. I'm not here to defeat anyone.

Q: Right now you are not speaking from the deep-deep sleep state. What are you speaking from?

K: I have no idea.

Q: Let's call it the Karl's state... [Laughter]

K: You can call it radi-Karl... [Laughter]

Q: But you have spoken about this before...

K: Yes. But I'm talking here now from the Shiva place, Shiva Shambhu, experiencing itself now as a conditioned and an unconditioned one. But the experience of unconditioned is still conditioned, but its Nature is still not conditioned or unconditioned. That quality I talk about only in this mountain and not about shamanism or (Carlos) Castaneda from New Mexico or somewhere else. I'm here in this place and it's resonating. So, I speak as it resonates.

Q: But hearing you talk about the seven stages...

K: First go to the second then we can talk further.

Q: The dream state...

K: They are all dream states. Even the fourth state is a dream state. That what is the Parabrahman is dreaming itself in all the seven different states and the fourth state is still a dream state. Even the natural state is a dream state.

Q: It depends...

K: The natural state depends on the state that is not natural. So it depends to be natural. Even depending to be natural is a dependency. Amazing!

Q: It's semantics...

K: Doesn't matter. It's all semantics anyway. I'm here to destroy everything, even destruction. You can use semantics and I cannot? I can only hit you with your own tools. [Laughter] If someone is loving here, I'm loving. If someone is semantic here, I'm semantic as well. If someone attacks, I attack back. I'm just resonating because I have no interest. No one can give me anything here. No one can make me more or less as I am. That I can only present, that I'm not here to please anyone. This carelessness, this helplessness is what I present. That even being What I am, I cannot decide where I sit because who wants to sit here? Not Karl. That I can present but not any explanation. I don't want to add any concept to all the concepts that you already have. Everyone is full of concepts anyway and I'm not here to feed that. I'm not in a zoo to feed the beast. I talk directly to the beast and tame the bull.

All the pointers can only point to the absolute absence of one who knows or doesn't know that which is Knowledge itself, which never needs to know itself. That which is independent knowledge, not depending on anyone that knows or doesn't know. That's the pointer. Deep-deep sleep is a pointer to That which is present even in the absence of the presence of the one who knows or doesn't know what it is. And That never needs to know itself to be Itself. The Absolute Self doesn't need to know the Self to be the Self, that's all! These are pointers to That what doesn't need anything. That is satisfaction itself in nature. That's why it's called *chit* or *sat*. But it doesn't need to *know sat*. *Ananda* doesn't need to know *ananda* to be *ananda*. The sweetness doesn't need to know the sweetness to be the sweetness. It doesn't need to taste itself. Knowledge doesn't need to taste knowledge to *be* knowledge and that what needs to taste knowledge, is false. It's a depending knowledge, that's all! But if you're interested in depending knowledge, go for it. But it will not satisfy you, that's all. Satisfaction is there only in being What-you-are and not as what you become.

Q: I suppose I'm trying to understand the genesis of the phantom. That what is in deep-deep sleep doesn't remain in this state?

K: That what you are in deep-deep sleep is that what you are now. It's not something different.

Q: You say that the fundamental nature of deep-deep sleep persists, but the sleeper awakes. What is that?

K: Deep-deep sleep is a dreamless state.

Q: Is the person awake there?

K: There is no person there. In the dream state even, there has to be a 'I' who's dreaming. But the 'I' is part of the dream. But That what is dreaming the dreamer, dreaming and what can be dreamt... cannot be dreamt! That what is imagining everything, realizing everything, dreamer, dreaming what can be dreamt... *cannot* be realized in the dream.

Q: And that never wakes up?

K: It neither wakes up or goes to sleep. It is Reality.

Q: That's good. I finally moved you one centimeter. I'm happy. That's enough for today. [Laughter]

Q [Another visitor]: You said something remains in deep-deep sleep?

K: No. I said that what you are is in deep-deep sleep That What-it-is but nothing remains there. Just the void remains.

Q: So, it's still something...

K: There is no 'something'. There's no God in that.

Q: Let me finish...

K: I'm here to finish you!

Q: For me when I sleep and I wake up...

K: Where's the 'me' in deep-deep sleep?

Q: When I fall asleep...

K: But you don't fall asleep...

Q: Let me finish...

K: You start wrong.

Q: Why?

K: The body drops away as an experience but you don't fall asleep and you still remain as you are.

Q: How do you know this? Because this is my experience not yours... [Laughter]

K: If you don't trust me, you can leave. You want to make it *your* experience and I'm not interested in you... especially not in your story.

Q: But it's not a story...

K: Of course it's a story – When 'I' fall asleep. It's a story.

Q: Alright. Sleep happens...

K: Sleep doesn't happen. [Laughter]

Q: I was waiting for four days for this question and now this... [Laughter]

K: [Laughing] Should I really show pity here? So when the dropping of the body happens and then I'm without the body...

Q: I cannot say...

K: But I tell you what happens. The world that comes with the body disappears when the body drops to sleep and you still remain what you are. You just turn to the other side of your being; to the absence. You turn from the presence to the absence – that's called sleep.

Q: So, I have to believe you?

K: You don't have to believe me, just try it out.

Q: But this is a statement, I cannot say it is like this...

K: But I say it because I'm sitting here and you there. [Laughter] Come on, if you don't trust what I say, you should go.

Q: But I don't want to go...

K: Then believe me! [Laughter]

Q [Another visitor]: But you said, you cannot tell us anything...

K: I said I cannot make you more or less as you are. I can tell you everything but it doesn't make you more or less as you are – that's what I said. But you remember it that way and whoever remembers me is wrong – even me. [Laughter] If I remember me, I'm wrong.

With the dropping of the body experience, the whole world disappears and you just turn to the absence. But the universe is not gone, the presence is not gone. Your perception disconnects from the presence and goes to the absence. That is what you call sleep. But there's no sleep in it, it's just an absence of experience. And what you are is still what it is. You now experience yourself as a presence and at night there's an absence. So you are in the presence and in the absence What-you-are, and That is never asleep or awake. It's just What-you-are, that being you cannot not be. That being is in the presence What-it-is and in the absence What-it-is. So, with 'you' the presence and the absence starts. But you are never-never. So, no one falls asleep.

Q: What wakes up?

K: There's no waking up. You didn't listen again! [Laughter] I try very hard and then comes this question.

Q: But there's an experience of waking up...

K: There's just a presence, a reference point of a 'me'. But the presence can only be there where there is a reference point of a 'me'... a seer who sees and then defines the world... and without that, there is nothing.

Q [Another visitor]: It seems like a reflection…

K: It's a dream-like experience but a false experience of waking up doesn't make it true.

Q [Another visitor]: But doesn't the 'I' wake up?

K: The 'I' doesn't wake up. The 'I' is still there waiting for you to give attention to it.

Q [Another visitor]: But you cannot avoid it…

K: I didn't say that. What are you defending now?

Q: It's a question…

K: It's not a question, you just made a statement. You need to have a question-mark after that. [Laughter]

Q: For some reason a reflection seems to arise…

K: You fall in love with the 'I' again which waits for your attention so that it exists, because without attention it doesn't exist. Your love for the imaginary 'I' makes you blind. You're blinded by the light – totally blind. You fall in love with the first light, the first awareness, which is already presence. But it is not That what you are. Then you fall in love with the first experience of the light of Shiva and then Shiva becomes a jiva by falling in love with its own light – an imaginary light! Then it claims that this awareness is better than the darkness. Instantly he has a preference because it's so in love with this imaginary light. Now you know. [Laughter]

Q [Another visitor]: Unavoidable…

K: Yeah. You cannot avoid falling in love. But you have to be the same as you are in the absence of it. You're not *depending* on that love – that's all. You *realize* yourself in a love affair. The presence is a love affair with yourself but you are That even in the absence of a love affair – that's all! You experience yourself as a lover, loving and as the beloved and the absence of a lover, loving and the beloved. So you are That what you don't know. You call that your Nature: the Nature realizing itself as a lover, loving and the beloved and in the absence of it. So, your Nature is not depending on the presence of a lover, loving and the beloved and how this love affair is. Your Nature doesn't depend on the way you love yourself or if it's a nice love or a fulfilling love, because satisfaction is even in the presence as it is in the absence That What-you-are.

That is satisfaction! The fact that you are in the presence as in the absence... Whatever it is, not depending on anything. Om Namah Shivaya.

Q [Another visitor]: Who is this 'I' that falls in love every morning?

K: There is no 'I' in it. There's just Parabrahman falling in love with Brahman, with this imaginary image. You cannot give it a name at all. It's That what you are which doesn't need a name; call it Heart, call it whatever. The Heart of existence, that which is the Absolute Being falls in love. Maybe the Absolute being is Love realizing itself as a lover, loving and the beloved. But it is *not* the lover, *not* the loving and *not* the beloved. That is the *realization* of Reality but not the Reality! The Reality is in the *absence* of the presence and in the *presence* of the presence That what is Reality, and it is not depending on any side.

You are the coin that has two sides. The coin never gets more or less as it is. You are the presence side and the absence. Even in shamanism there is *nagual* and *tonal* – that what is information and the non-information. The absolute absence of any imaginary thing and the presence of it. But none of that makes you more or less, that's the main thing. You have nothing to gain or to lose in the presence or in the absence. You are Absolute in whatever way. And you can make it personal or impersonal, it doesn't matter. By personal you don't lose anything and by impersonal you don't gain anything. There's no gaining or losing in anything. You can experience yourself as the most personal and the biggest bullshitter but it doesn't make you less. If you experience yourself in the highest Samadhi, you are still What-you-are. All those seven states is a dream, none of that makes you more or less as you are. But That what you are, you will never know.

Q [Another visitor]: But when I wake up, there is this talking personality...

K: So what? Does it make you less? Be the fucker, the fucking and the fucked. You *are* it anyway! You are the raper, the raping and the raped! And being raped by yourself, what is there to complain? You can even be the complainer, complaining and that what is being complained. Even complaining doesn't make you less! That's why Ramana's famous statement is 'Be as you are. It doesn't say be *what* you are. 'Be as you are' means be *Absolute*! And you cannot get less or more Absolute. There is no less or more Absolute; Absolute is *Absolute*! That's the noumenon in Nature. And the Absolute doesn't need to know the Absolute to be the Absolute, that's the nature of the Absolute – finished! [Laughter]

Q [Another visitor]: But Karl...

K: There is no but Karl. [Laughter]

Q: But the absence cannot be known, it cannot be experienced...

K: Of course it can be known. Every night you experience the absence. The Absolute experiencer is experiencing the absence of the experiencer. So, even the absence of an experience is an experience.

Q: But can you experience it?

K: There is no 'you' but still What-you-are is still there. You really claim that you are needed to exist? You think Existence needs *you* to exist? You believe so. This arrogance is where you are talking from and that makes you suffer. This arrogance that the world needs you to be. That Existence needs your presence so that Existence can be. Ha ha ha! How big you are!

Q: But the experience is that there is no experience...

K: No experience is *still* an experience.

Q [Another visitor]: For whom?

K: For you!

Q: But I don't exist there...

K: [Pointing to both the visitors] Both of you can marry. [Laughter] Then one can be awake all the time and the other one asleep. They really want to make it a personal bullshit. It's amazing! I'm talking here from whatever and then comes [Mocking] 'But Karl there's no 'me' and nothing exists when I'm not there. [Laughter] I'm God and I feel that without me, nothing is! Only when I am there's something and I need to experience myself so that there's something. If I don't experience myself, there cannot be anything'. Amazing! What arrogance speaks! That arrogance is pitiful and self-important and that makes you suffer. It's amazing! Then they get punished just by being arrogant, because by that you are not What-you-are. Because by that you are something what can be known and that is already a punishment! That's why it's called the u-punish-ads. [Laughter] And yoga fascista! [Laughter]

This is fascism. This is a little Hitler who thinks that he is needed so that the world can exist. That the 'me' is needed for Existence to exist... that's the arrogance of this mind. When 'I' am not, nothing can be. And you will be surprised! Existence still *is* without 'me'... imagine! It is a typical thing that one believes that he is the centre of the universe and without 'me' nothing can be... fantastic! It has to be like a story, you have to be there so that you can count. [Mocking] 'If I am not there, it doesn't count for me. What do I get out of it if I'm not there? What is my advantage if I'm not there? I want to *experience* that I'm not there'. [Laughter] You will be amazed, that What-you-are even exists without you. Then you better be what you cannot not be, because it exists with and *without* you. That's the only pointer! That what is *with* and *without* you has nothing to gain with you or nothing to lose without you.

So you can be very generous about this little guest. Waking up in the morning, the experience of the guest comes and at night the experience of the guest goes. So be my guest... that's all! You can be generous because you have nothing to gain or to lose with whatever the guest is guessing. Let the guest guess whatever he's guessing!

But the guest becomes king-like and says – 'I am the King, this is my Universe'. You can allow him, let him be King for a while. It's like a fool who wants to be a king, a ghost who likes to be a king, an imaginary experience who likes to be the king... 'Because I exist you have to support me, Existence must take care of me!'

Fantastic! All the esoteric ideas come now from the guest... that I exist now so the kingdom has to support me. Since I'm looking for truth, Existence must support my famous search for my Nature. Come on Existence! Give me something! [Laughter] Maybe I pray and bow down to you, but then you have to give me something. Come on! Because I'm That and I want something from you, so now you have to deliver. This is a self-deliverance and I have given an order to the universe. Now you deliver, please! Come, come, come...

It's like one person meditates like hell for enlightenment but his neighbour gets it. [Laughter] Then the one who delivers the enlightenment from above says – Oops, sorry again! I missed again because my eye-sight is really bad today. Then the one who gets enlightened doesn't know what to do with it... Suddenly he's enlightened! Then he says, 'This is not my beautiful wife, this is not my car, this is not my house'. Then he ends up in a mad house! And the neighbour who could use this enlightenment, gets a new Mercedes [Laughter] but he cannot drive it because he has no license. What a joke! All these mad houses are full of enlightened ones who cannot use it and all the ones in ashrams don't get it because they want it. The Universal Personal System (UPS) delivers on the wrong address. And there are some times when the UPS is right where it has to be.

It's never fair. One strives for it for the whole lifetime and is very earnest but then the wife gets it. [Laughter] That's the most unfair thing. The one who always complained that you are never at home, you are meditating all the time, you're never seen, *gets* it! Now what to do with an enlightened woman? That's what you'd call a worst case scenario! The Buddha promised that women can never get enlightened. But look, even the impossible is possible!

Q: I say one word and you say one thousand. I'm not able to say anything...

K: Then you should rent your own rooftop and wait if someone comes. [Laughter] Complaining that he cannot talk enough here. But for that you have to rent a room, *then* you can talk.

... Anyone remembers what I was saying?

Q [Another visitor]: You were talking about women getting enlightened and that's the worst case scenario...

K: That's the worst case scenario; to have a woman who is enlightened. She knows everything! [Laughter]

Q: But she doesn't bother...

K: But she still knows! That's worse, a woman who doesn't bother, doesn't cook. You come home and you have to do everything yourself! So make sure to keep your wife busy with something else... Give her your Gold credit card for shopping. [Laughter] Shopping mall is the biggest religion in America... shop until you drop!

Q [Another visitor]: I wonder if self-inquiry with the mind and without any heart has any value...

K: I *hope* it has no value. I have no interest in a personal heart! There are too many therapists sitting somewhere having interest in personal heart. This is not a therapy. I cannot heal you.

Q: If I talk from the direct path of experience, I was broken and I failed. Then I was sitting in a cafe in south India. For some reason I sat on the same table and same chair for many days and for no reason I found myself contemplating about love, I don't know why. Then came this beautiful Indian family...

K: Make it shorter, I'm already bored with the story... 'My experience of love in South India'.

Q: What you are saying is also just another...

K: If you don't like it, you don't have to listen to it.

Q: I'm just inquiring...

K: You're not inquiring, you just want to tell a story of love and comparing something. You're making *that* better than something else, that's what you try to do. It's all a personal story... 'Then I had love and it was all so bearable'. I hear it all the time around the world and I'm not interested in personal stories.

Q: And you say whatever your mind wants to say...

K: And then the 'love' people start offending others – 'You talk out of mind and I talk out of heart. It's amazing! Always making a discrimination between mind and heart and I'm a heart person and you're a mind person. It's fantastic how these heart people offend everyone. I really hate them. [Laughter] They're permanently offending people by saying you're only in your mind and I'm in my heart.

Q: Just like you say my heart thing bores you, is the same as me saying your mind things bore me. Neither of these is true, so why are you heading this way because it was not really such a long story...

K: It was a very long story, ask anybody. 'Me' sitting on the table, 'me' had an experience. I'm not here to harm you, I just point it out. And if that really would be true, you would be permanently in that, you would not stand here. If that was your real experience, you would not stand here and talk about it. You can only talk about stories which are really not important.

Q: So it was just a fiction?

K: It was a fiction for sure. Every emotion is fiction.

Q: This wasn't about emotion...

K: It *is* emotion because now you make a story out of it. The mind makes a story out of everything. Even the deepest heart experience and love and things, it always makes shit out of it.

Q: It wasn't about a personal love story...

K: But even saying it was not personal, makes something that is personal as shit! You confirm that personal is shit and impersonal is *not* shit and that is mind. Who makes a difference?

Q: It is just a clever argument...

K: Call it whatever... You see? I just try to point it out and you try to offend me. Why do you need to attack from that point of heart? If there really *would* be love and heart, why is there an attack from it? Why are you defending it?

Q: I just point it back to you as you point it to me...

K: If you don't like it, just go.

Q: I'm just checking here...

K: ...and I don't want checkers here. I'm not interested in checkers.

Q: Why say anything at all?

K: People like to listen to me and if one doesn't like it, one can go.

Q: I do realize that I can go at any point in time...

K: You think? Then go – prove it. [Laughter]

Q: Why should I need to go?

Q [Another visitor]: We come for him [pointing to Karl] and not for you...

K: Any one else who wants to listen to me? [Laughter]

Q [Another visitor]: You made a flat statement that if women get enlightened, they stop cooking? [Laughter] I'd like to challenge that.

K: They still may be cooking but there is no *cook* left! [Laughter] That's the meaning of enlightenment, there's cooking but without a cook. When I say there's no cooking wife, I mean there may be cooking left but no cook. So, cooking may continue. Talking may continue but there's no one who talks. But the tendency of the wife may continue in the same way, nothing has to change for it. And if there's a change, it's not because of enlightenment. There's no side-effect of enlightenment. There's no influence of this dream.

PEACE OFF: AND BE WHAT YOU ARE

There's no advantage of disadvantage by enlightenment. The absolute advantage of enlightenment is that you are That which never needs any advantage at all! I can only point to it and maybe that's what you are longing for. But that's what you are. Being That what never needs any advantage is being What-you-are. And whatever needs an advantage, is a ghost advantage. It's like a phantom advantage and the phantom who claims to be enlightened or has any idea of anything is a phantom enlightenment and for sure doesn't count! And an enlightenment that produces an enlightened one for sure was not enlightenment. Realization that leaves one who is realized, is not realization!

And I can just point to it, I cannot make you feel it because this is not something you can feel. It's not about feeling or anything. This is being What-you-are which is in the presence and absence of any story What-it-is, and not because of any deep or high what you can remember. Because What-you-are doesn't need to re-member itself. It's never a member of anything. The Self has no relationship, even to Itself! There's no relationship to anything. And all we can talk about in mind and words and love, needs relationship. There has to be a lover and a beloved, but for What-you-are, there's no lover and no beloved in Reality. You are That what is with and without the story of a lover and a beloved What-it-is. So, what to do?

So, I don't want to change anything. Let there be heart or not, good or bad and all those emotional stories is fine. But it's not fine enough for you. It's all wonderful, but not the wonder you are! When I say I cannot *make* you that, I mean it! And I cannot give you any heart because you are already that Heart. And That never needs to experience itself. But the heart you own always needs a confirmation, okay? Why not? You can be very generous, as you are that anyway because there's nothing to gain or lose in all those stories. That's why I call it his-story. This is his-story, but What-you-are never has any story, and by none of these stories you can lose or gain yourself. And you cannot get lost in it and you cannot go back from it. You were never lost in anything, how can you go back to anything? What is there to do? You never *unlearnt* to exist, so how can you learn to exist?

But now you believe that you have to learn that Existence you are. That you can train yourself to be That or you have to have a special experience for that. No! The Absolute Experience you are is uninterrupted in the presence and in the absence. You are Heart in the presence and in the absence of whatever you imagine. But that you cannot imagine, because that Heart you are, you cannot imagine. And That cannot be owned by anyone. There is no 'my' heart in that. There's no 'my' love. There's no concept of love in That What-you-are. And that is satisfaction in Nature, which is not satisfied by any event or any story. It is uninterrupted What-you-are and not because of something.

Of course, this sounds like mind and intellectual. But how else can you talk? Silence is the best. But I have to talk so that the silence can be. When there's this talk, then there's a listening without a listener so that silence can just be. I keep you busy in your belief system so that What-you-are can be What-it-is. So, I agree that I talk to the mind, but the mind never minds. And never-mind is the absence of the mind. So I try my best but it's never good enough, I know. But for me that's good enough- that nothing is good enough.

Q [Another visitor]: From the relative point of view it seems to have advantages - like there's no fear. It seems like an advantage to me...

K: And I have nothing against people who make it a therapy.

Q: I'm not talking about therapy...

K: But this is therapy – trying to make your life better. More peaceful, that's therapy.

Q: Sometimes you say there is no fear...

K: No. I say there's fearlessness that experiences fear. Otherwise I wouldn't have jumped away from the snake. I don't *fear* the fear – that's all! What I am doesn't fear the fear. What I am never fears anything. So, I don't fear the fear; let there be fear. Who fears fear?

Who has this angst against the angst? Nothing can make you more or less as you are. That is what can never get sick by anything. That what now needs to be healed by some love and therapy... who cares? It's a story of a disease.

Ramana mentioned it too, this body is a sickness, a disease. It came and it will be gone one day and What I am is neither sick nor not sick. It is just that What-it-is. That never needs any cure. That is what you are longing for. But still you can have a nice life, go for Ayurveda or do Reiki. You can even be rich and still you are What-you-are... imagine! That's impossible normally, that you're wealthy, rich, have a Mercedes, a good wife and a good relationship. And you still can be What-you-are. [Laughter] It's amazing! Actually unbelievable.

Many believe that they have to be a *brahmachari* with nothing around, having a very simple life, living in Himalayas and maybe *then* I become what I am. By reducing myself to the minimum, then I come closer to what I am. No! You are *further* away by that... it's really not fair. Even Mr. Trump is What he is. [Laughter] It's not fair!

Around ten years ago I told this story to someone that you are Consciousness in action, you are Hitler, you played the concentration camp, you're the most hating and the most loving, you are the evil, the devil, and you are even Andrew Cohen. That was the limit. [Laughter] One person rose up and he was a Jew from Israel and he said, 'Karl I can be Hitler, no problem. I can be a concentration camp guard, I can be whatever you said but not Andrew Cohen [Laughter] Now you went too far!'

All the understanding has limits. Even the loving heart that you think you have, has limits. All those things are limited. But the Heart you *are* has no such thing. There's no limit for the Heart you are. But the heart you *have*, this loving caring thing, has limits! You can accept everything, agree to everything but maybe your neighbour is too much. [Laughter] There's always something that's too much, you'll find it sooner or later. Your acceptance will break.

But the acceptance of Heart, which is What-you-are, which never needs to accept anything, is unbreakable! There's no need for acceptance of that what is Acceptance. And there's no need for love for that what *is* Love. I can only point to that! And being that is your very nature, your natural state, because Love doesn't need love and Peace doesn't need peace. And that what needs peace is okay but it's never good enough! Then you fight for peace, you fight for love, you fight for that. All the wars come from fighting for a good reason.

But for the Heart you are, you don't have to fight. You don't have to defend it. There's nothing to defend. There's no armour needed for What-you-are. But for any idea, any concept, you have to defend, you need an armour around it. You have to defend it, you have to make it stable. You have to create a stronghold so that it can withstand attacks. So, what to do?

What-you-are never needs a defenc e system and what you believe to be has to defend itself permanently. It always has to defend and everyone I meet is really tired about it – 'I'm so tired about defending myself, so fed up! Even the love idea, I have to defend and I'm so tired about it because the result is the opposite of what I want. I had such a good intention but the result is so bad – failing, failing, failing!' But to be What-you-are, you never fail. So be That what never fails, because you cannot fail to be What-you-are. But with everything else, you fail – everything! Fantastic!

That's called a Buddha. He didn't *become* a Buddha, he was a Buddha *already*! Just the idea that he could do something, he could become something, dropped. And he was That what he was before, during and after that. Nothing ever happened to That what he is! Being That is helplessness, you cannot change anything because you're not part of it. You're the Almighty, the energy Itself, that what is the Almighty Dreamer but you cannot change your dream. The dream is already dreamt, you're the Absolute potential of all beings, the whole universe, the whole existence, but by being that, you cannot change What-you-are. Even as the Absolute potential, the dream is already finished!

That's what Krishna says in the Mahabharata – Even me who created the whole blueprint of existence, cannot change a single thing out of it. You have to go to war, you have to kill your friends and enemies – if you like it or not. Even I who created the whole blueprint of existence, cannot change any single aspect of it. This helplessness! You have to realize yourself as you are – Absolute as you are. There's no way of changing anything because you're that what is the Unchangeable... even in your realization.

That's peace! And for me that peace is incomparable. And that peace doesn't come by loving or it doesn't go by hating. That's why I like the peace you are. That's why it's called Shanti, Shanti, Shanti. So, I'm peace-fool. [Laughter] That what is Peace shows itself in everything, even in attacking and war. It cannot decide how it realizes itself – even as Mr. Trump. It's amazing! Otherwise would you think God would allow Mr. Trump to happen if God had a choice? [Laughter] I think everyone would agree, if God had a choice and a little taste, would he allow a guy like Mr. Trump or Hitler to exist? If there really would be a God who has taste for love, would these guys even pop up? If really God could help himself?

So, you have to realize yourself and you cannot decide how. Total helplessness! You have to be... in spite of the way you realize yourself... that Peace you *are* and not because there's peace in the world or peace in your mind. So, peace off! And be the Peace you are, because that peace could never be destroyed and never would be disturbed by anything. And I can only point out that the false peace you can reach, can be disturbed again, so it cannot be the peace you're longing for. Being What-you-are is peace and you cannot not be it, so be it! And none of these events could disturb the Peace you are or can make it more or less as it is.

I can only point to it but I cannot give it to you. I cannot give you what you already are – you have to *be* it. *You* have to be it! It doesn't matter if I'm it or not, you have to be it for what you are. Don't look at me. It's all about this one, That what is your nature, that which is your natural state which is peace. The Peace which is not dependent on any outside peace or war or anything. No one can be it for you, not even me. And I don't want to be it for you.

Q [Another visitor]: The resistance and fear is too strong. It does not allow me to go where you're pointing to…

K: You're still in love with this body. You're Rama and where there's Rama there's drama! That's the nature of Rama. When Rama knows Rama there's drama. No, you cannot stop it. Who *needs* to stop it? That's the question! Is That What-you-are disturbed by it? No! It's only that what is an idea that is disturbed by other ideas. What is in for you if it stops? Who needs that advantage that it stops? Say it, pronounce it… 'me'! It's always 'me' and that 'me' is the root of misery and meanings and mine and everything.

What is this 'me'? A phantom. The phantom needs survival, it needs whatever. He needs to suffer because without suffering it doesn't exist. So you take care about your suffering. You make *sure* that you suffer because only in suffering you exist, only in disturbance you can exist. In harmony you cannot exist. So, you do your best to create disturbance so that you can exist. When there would be harmony, when there would be peace, you cannot remain as what you are, so you try to survive and you can only survive in disharmony. That's the nature of 'me', you cannot exist in harmony. Every night when you shut up, the harmony starts… because when you are, harmony cannot be. And every morning the disharmony wakes up. The body already is a disharmony. It's a discomfort experience. Then comes the story of disharmony: then you try to bring harmony to disharmony, that's your daily work. Daily trying to work, trying to cure yourself, trying to be in harmony with this body, taking care about it only so that it doesn't disturb you. But taking care that it doesn't disturb you, creates the disturbance. You give attention to the body because you think the body should not disturb you to be healthy.

The tricks are so immense. The so-called mind or 'me' is the biggest trickster you can imagine because in the nature it is not different as Absolute. So, his nature is Absolute and its tricks are

Absolute. This trapper who always creates the traps for himself creates traps for that what he is and his Absolute traps you cannot avoid. Even *trying* to avoid the trap becomes the next trap! Even *not* stepping in the next trap, is the next trap! Thinking that you're clever enough and 'I don't make the mistake again' is the next mistake!

You're always mistaken. You take yourself as something what you're not. It's always a mis-take and in the mistake you miss yourself. You have to be That what never makes any mistake, never takes anything as what it is. But that what takes himself as something, is a mistake. Then you become a 'me' steak. That's the biggest mistake that this 'me' is a steak. I take myself as a body – that's the *biggest* mistake. Then something is at stake for that steak. [Laughter] I love English, as a German it's amazing! I like to play with it.

But taking this steak as you, the mistake continues. The first step is that you see that you're not the body. The second step is when you see this as your experience. For that you make Zazen sittings. You sit so long and it becomes so uncomfortable that you disconnect from this body. Then you enter the space-like I Amness. Then comes the next state. You look everywhere for comfort and when you have gone through all the seven states and could not find it, you remain as that What-you-are which never needs comfort to be. And that's the comfort of Existence that doesn't need comfort in anything. Take comfort in That what doesn't need to experience comfort!

I approach it from many ways and I try my best but it may not work. What to do? And if I say no experience can make you What-you-are, you can believe it or not – but you can try. You have to look for yourself. Don't trust me, trust only that inner guru you are. If that tells you look there, go there, go for it! ...and find out for yourself that it is not there. If I tell you it's not there, it doesn't matter. You have to go yourself into that. You have to go through all of that. I can say a lot, I can say it all doesn't work but you have to go there anyway. So, go!

That's the ultimate medicine. Go through all that and try your best, but it will never be good enough and *that* you have to find out yourself! Don't trust anyone else. You're all experts here. You went through so many experiences and insights and outsides and clarities and unclarities and things and techniques. You failed so many times already but who knows when the final failure happens? It can be in the next moment or in a thousand years. But it will happen – that I promise you. Absolutely!

It's like two sadhus sitting under the tree and Narada passes by. One sadhu asks him – 'When will I get enlightened?' Narada says, 'You will be enlightened in as many lifetimes as there are leaves on this tree'. Then the first sadhu was angry and depressed. But when the second sadhu heard the same news, he was thrilled – 'I will be enlightened! Who cares when?' So, everyone is already enlightened but who cares when? It is already there and will happen in whatever time. But the other one is impatient – I want it now. It doesn't happen in 'now' because 'now' is too late! [Laughter] I can only be a fool for myself, talking to the Kingdom and not the king – that I can do. What to do?

So, I say enlightenment is unavoidable. Whatever you do or don't do, it will happen anyway. But you have to do your best.

Q [Another visitor]: What do you mean by – do your best?

K: Do whatever you do, you'll always do your best. You can only do your best! Can you do something else other than your best? [Laughter] So do your best!

Q [Another visitor]: You spoke about the impatience...

K: That's the passion of Christ.

Q: But you also say that you have to be like a man ten feet under water...

K: Until that happens, you have to be patient. [Laughter] If you by your so-called free will dive, and you know that you can go up whenever you like, it doesn't work! It will put you down and the choicelessness and the helplessness will be there and not by you diving and thinking – I made it. I'm now ten meters under water. Come on now, make me enlightened! [Laughter]

You're *already* in the tiger's mouth but you never know when it eats you. The tiger is always there. It already has you because you already give your attention to That what you are. You're already in the tiger's mouth and it will swallow you. You will be swallowed and the tiger will remain as a tiger. That's what Papaji says, 'Wake up and roar!' Be That what is the tiger and not what needs to be swallowed. You can already *be* the tiger and this is in your mouth. It doesn't matter when you eat this little guy, it will be eaten. You're *beyond* eaten. [Laughter]

Q [Another visitor]: You make jokes about Mooji...

K: I make jokes about everyone.

Q: Could you say something about Osho?

K: Once there was a show and now there's no-show! [Laughter] I only remember that my parents had sex for the first time when he got enlightened. [Laughter] And I came out of it. It was in March 1953 and I was born that December. I counted. [Laughter] That's why I never went to him. Because of that guy, I have to walk on this earth now. I talked a lot about him earlier. I'm always surrounded by Osho widows or Papaji widows. These are all widows, the guru dies and they start running around looking for another man. [Laughter] I have the tendency of attacking someone's guru and when he starts to defend him, he doubts him. The moment you defend your guru, you doubt him. I don't doubt anyone. I don't mind anyone, it's just for fun. But if you try to defend him, then he becomes small for you.

Sometimes in Bombay I try to attack Nisargadatta and they don't react. It's useless, there's no defence system running. But when I attack Osho, the defence system wakes up... 'You cannot say this about Osho, he gave me so much, all my practices, all my massage, I survive by them'. Some of them would be furious and say, 'You cannot talk about my guru like that'. I would say, 'Watch me!' [Laughter]

The pointer is that if it's meant to happen, it has to happen. And what is not meant to happen, it will not happen!

Q [Another visitor]: How can you say for sure that you are going to wake up?

K: I never said you'd wake up, I said you'd be enlightened – because you already are. [Laughter] It's for sure. Nothing is more sure than the fact that you're the Light itself. So, you will be enlightened. Every morning you're enlightened and you experience yourself as the light. This in nature is all light. This is all a vibration of light, you know that. Even the quantum physics, all the scientists all agree that this is all light. It is all a vibration of energy or light, call it whatever. You enlighten yourself every morning, when you turn your attention to that light you are. This is the light of Shiva, this Arunachala is the presence of light. You experience yourself already as light.

But you look for a *special* light, that's your problem. [Laughter] That's the one and only problem that you look for a special light and you want to make it 'your' light. You want to put it in your pocket and show it to your friends. But light cannot be stored somewhere. It's already everywhere. How can it be limited by whatever? That's why Brahma and Vishnu tried to find the end of the light and Brahma cheated. He claimed that he found the beginning of the light and for that there's only one temple of Brahma in whole of India and all the liars go there. [Laughter]

So, whoever claims that he found the end of his existence, that he realized his true nature, you can say – what a lie! Whoever claims that this is the true nature and that is not – lie! Whoever knows what is a lie and what is not a lie and what is the beginning and the end is a liar. And you're one of them.

But I still tell you, every moment you're enlightened… because this is an experience of light because Reality is realizing itself as light, in whatever way. Even mind is light. That's amazing! Even mind is light! Heart people would never agree to that! [Laughter] It's amazing! Even separation is light... Impossible! Everyone agrees that Oneness is light. I'm delighted by oneness. But separation? No, that cannot be light! The experience of separation cannot be light. I would never agree to that. [Mocking] I want Oneness, I want waves to come in. [Laughter] So much magnificence. [Pointing to a visitor] Now you get Osho! [Laughter]

In Germany when you're in a dark forest and you're alone then you start singing out of fear. That's like Bhajans [Laughter] I make jokes about everything. I don't spare anyone. In the seventies, I tried to get laughing gas in Germany and there was no laughing gas left because Osho took everything. [Laughter] There was a total shortage of laughing gas through the world because he was storing it in Poona. Just-in-case, he had halls full of laughing gas and the other hall was full of Valium.

That's why I like Osho a little bit. In seventies, whenever you went to a dentist, they gave you laughing gas and immediately you had an out-of-body experience. Even when I had no pain, I would ask my mum to take me to the dentist. [Laughter] So I understand why he was doing it all the time. It just disconnects your perception from your body. And if you can do it all the time, why not? If you have the possibility. Or take Valium for Shanti, peace. Ramana needed to work for five hours in a kitchen for that. That's another kind of Valium. He was so tired by seven in the morning and was resting. Then all the westerners woke up and went to the ashram and said – what a peaceful man! [Laughter] If they would've seen him as a tyrant in the kitchen, maybe their opinion would have been different.

There are two sides of Ramana and I like him for that. He was the most natural guy. You cannot say he was like this, he was everything. He was impatient, he was patient, he was this, he was that. I like Happy-Nappy. [Laughter] The symbol of the nappy points to the baby state. A baby who doesn't know what a baby is.

That's why everyone loves a baby because he's innocent. There's an innocence of a baby because the baby has no doership in it, no ownership. There's just What-you-are – the innocent state – his natural state. He walked around like a baby.

But I would not do that! [Laughter] Two weeks ago in Ashram there was a guru who was dressed in pampers and he walked around with a stick. Okay, have a good nap, with and without a nappy. Thank you for going... [Laughter]

2nd Feb 2016
Tiruvannamalai

Chapter Two

Be The Freedom That's Free From The Idea Of Freedom

Q: Why does Yama always appears with a dark scary face?

K: The Reaper is very jolly.

Q: It appears very scary...

K: For you, because you fear the reaper. But the Reaper is your best friend. It says, 'Hello what took you so long?' [Laughter]

Q: Why don't I recognize him?

K: Because you fear him, you turn away from him. Whenever he comes, you turn to the other side. You scream like the painting of [Edvard] Munch. It's really stupid to fear the best that can happen to you, to get rid of that disease. On the contrary you should be happy and ask the Reaper – Hallelujah! What took you so long? I was waiting for you so long.

Q: Why am I not happy to meet the Reaper?

K: Because you're so in-fucking love with your body, being French. That makes you fear the Reaper. Love makes you fear something.

But that is your only best friend, your one and only lover – death! You must say – I am death (That). [Laughter] You have to recognize yourself in death, in that what is the absence and not only in this bloody presence here. You're so fucking in love with this presence and you think that it can give you something. The absence takes away everything from you but as it does that, you are What-you-are. And you are not by the presence of whatever is here – *sat-shit-ananda*.

Shit! Shit! Shit! Shit! Shit! But you are so in love with this little shit here. This shit factory you believe to be in. This is a running shit factory, but you have to give a shit about that. So, see the shit as shit and be chit.

Good?

Q: No, it's good but it's not good…

K: Because she wants to control death. She wants to live forever. But she's afraid to live forever because she would not know what to do with it. Especially when you're old and your body is not so good anymore: you wait to die but you cannot, because you were eating well and not smoking. All that you had done to live longer, is now working against you. [Laughter] You lived like an ascetic, eating organic and then you get really old and you wished that you smoked and ate all that was bad for you because then you can say good bye easier. But now you're healthy and you have twenty years more to live. [Laughter] And there's no intention for sex anymore, so what should you do with all this time? [Laughter] Twenty more years of boredom. Start smoking, go to the living room. [Laughter] [Pointing to a visitor] She lives with a guy who's a chain smoker smoking two packs of cigarettes everyday and she has to sit in the kitchen. But I always tell her go to the living room. [Laughter] But she's sitting in the hell's kitchen, trying to stay healthy. That's why it's called a hell's kitchen.

Q: I want to die healthy…

K: She really has compassion for the worms. No worm should be sick after eating me. [Laughter]

Q: This thing is totally out of control...

K: Was there any control?

Q: No!

K: So what are you complaining about? But you're French so you have to complain sometimes otherwise you're not French anymore.

That's why when you age you go to Church because then you think that now I have to see him soon. Earlier, they say I don't need any God and later all become religious again and sit in the Church. [Laughter] I better behave now because the end is near.

Q: Just-in-case...

K: Just-in-case there's a God, I sit in front of him. [Laughter]. I'm here. I was brave, not always. But now...

Q: The death of this body is not there before the death of the body...

K: You have to let the dead die... only *dead* can die! Now you think that really there's a dying that happens. Meditating on death is the *real* meditation, meditating on the absence permanently! Then seeing that even in the absence you are still What-you-are. For you there's no such thing as death. There's no life and there's no death. You have to meditate twenty-four by seven on death. So, let the dead die because you're still What-you-are in any absence of one who is and one who is not. So, death cannot touch you; as you are not born. As death dies, birth dies too – instantly!

So, don't meditate on peace or anything, meditate on death. And not with closed eyes because the inner direction is looking in front of you. The absence of the presence is not somewhere inside. You're the Absolute seer and now you look at the presence only. But in the presence and the absence, there's no two. The dead is already there, as the absence is already there. It's not like an insight or beyond or prior.

No. Here-now, you're the Absolute Seer! This is your presence and the nature of this presence is the absence. So, the presence and absence are not two. There's death and life right now. Here! Not somewhere else. Not in two years or five years or ten years. There is death and life, now. These are the two faces of Shiva. It's not some future bullshit. So, meditate! Now, I get really soft. [Laughter]

That is the nature of meditation, that you face the Infinite because death shows you the infinite. The Absolute absence where Jesus went – to the kingdom of the dead. There's a kingdom of life and there's a kingdom of the dead: but both kingdoms are What-you-are. So, you're in the kingdom of life and in the kingdom of death That what is the kingdom of Heart... because you're That what is the Heart of life and the Heart of death. So, you meditate on death. Now you only experience whatever is present.

Q [Another visitor]: Can you recommend the ways to meditate on death?

K: I just explained that. A few days ago I pointed it out. You have two hands. You put the hands like this [Joining both the palms together straight out in front of the body with the forefingers touching]. First you get comfortable, say fuck it all [Laughter] then look at where the two fingers meet. Then you [stretching his arms horizontally] and you still look at the imaginary point where the fingers met because there's nothing to look at anymore. Then you look at the nothingness or emptiness. You're the zero! Then you [Joining the hands in front] look at the presence and then [Stretching the arms wide] you look at the absence. It's not closing your eyes and trying to find peace in mind. There's no peace in mind, there's only Peace which is already there... which is the presence and the absence. You can call the absence as the God particle, which is everywhere. The moment when you concentrate only on that point, then you expand into the infinite – instantly. And that's meditation. It's not trying to find a little personal peace... *my* peaceful mind!

Q [Another visitor]: I tried that but it gave me a headache...

K: Because you want to survive, that gives you the headache – because you concentrate. You just have to relax in it. You want something from it. That gives you a headache. But meditation is meditation without expectation. It's not trying to get better there or trying to find peace in the absence. You cannot survive in the absence but you *want* to survive in the absence. You want to make it *your* peace and by that you get a headache. That's the punishment you deserve. [Laughter]

If you want to control peace, even the absence, you get a headache. You cannot, it's unbearable! But you try and then your nervous system collapses. You have to relax in that. But how to do that? You cannot relax by trying to relax... relaxation happens. You have to try and relax on that point for a long time and one day Satori will happen. This is Zazen. You sit in front of an imaginary wall and you concentrate on that point. At one point there's a Satori of an opening to that what is the Holy Spirit – the Infinite – which is everywhere and nowhere. The centreless centre. That's Zazen. But now you're looking at, whatever... 'Now I become Zen.' [Laughter]

Q [Another visitor]: But if you're focusing on a particular imaginary point, it becomes a concentration, isn't it?

K: No, it's not. Only when you want something from it. You put yourself in a concentration camp and you're the guard who wants to guard, because you want to survive. You even want to survive in the absence, that makes you a concentration camp. You fear the absence and by that you want to stay in the presence. But by trying to stay in the presence, you get exhausted and have a headache. There's no 'why' in it! Because you want something, the punishment is that you get punishment by headache and pain.

Q [Another visitor]: But the moment you do this [stretching the arms out in front]...

K: There's no *moment*... this is not a 'doing'! This is just being That what is the presence and the absence.

Q: But why do I have to do this stupid thing?

K: Because you want to burn in the light of the absence, that's why! Now she makes this pointer as a stupid thing as well. She says, why should I meditate? What do I get out of it? The business lady starts again, 'Why should I do that? I'm the Queen of existence, why should I do something to *get* something?' If you don't need it, don't do it... so, fuck off! Why do I talk to you? Tell me! Or to anyone for that matter. Why am I doing that? To get attacked here by stupid things? Fuck off! [Laughter]

Q [Another visitor]: My doctor once told me that I had a particular type of cancer. I went to Google and checked and basically I found that there's nothing you can do about it. Then there was peace. The next day the doctor mentioned that there was hope of finding a cure. A part of me was really pissed that there was hope again...

K: I have many friends who had the same experience. The moment the doctor said you'd die next month, they were totally in peace. The moment doctors tell them that we can make an operation and you can live again for four or five years, the whole fucking mind starts again – my insurance, my car, my daughter. The whole personal bullshit comes back again. I always tell you, you're already dead, don't worry. I confirm you you're already dead. So, you can relax now. [Laughter] You don't have to postpone that and you don't need a doctor who gives you a report for that. I confirm you now and forever, you're dead.

Q [Another visitor]: Then you say, rest in peace...

K: You have to make a tattoo when you're alive – Rest in peace. You're a walking tombstone with a tattoo – Rest in peace! I'm not the first one who says that the moment you're born, you've got a life sentence, and on top of it a death penalty! [Laughter] It's a double penalty when you believe you're born, then you have a life sentence and a death penalty which waits for you. And on the day of execution, nothing happens again! It's all for nothing. You sit in prison for nothing. You don't even know for what. But you always want to find out, why am I here? Why do I have to be in this body?

You want to find out what have I done wrong last time so that I have to come back again? The whole incarnation idea comes from what they have done last time because of which now they have *this* life.

So, what to do? How to stop the wheel of reincarnation? How can you stop what never moved? That's the problem because there was never anyone born in the first place! So how can you stop that what never happened? Tell me! How can you end something that has no beginning? Try! So, what to do? Let die what can die and let live what can live and be That what doesn't have to live in living and cannot die in dying. That is not something you can learn or attain or anything. But any moment you believe that you have a body, you exist, then you're fucked! What to do? Then trying *not* to be born again, you're born already! So, now it's too late! Whatever you try to stop this wheel of reincarnation confirms that there's one who's incarnated. It's a trick! Now by trying *not* to come back, you're here and you confirm the one who's born! By trying *not* to be born, you're already born now. What a trap! Now trying to get out of it is even worse. It's too late! So, what to do? Crucify me!

Do whatever you like or don't...it's all fiction anyway! From fiction to fiction - science fiction!

Q: It's freedom...

K: That's another fiction! You better be free from freedom and be What-you-are because What-you-are doesn't need any freedom. And that what needs freedom is imprisoned by the idea of freedom. Fuck freedom and be What-you-are!

Q [Another visitor]: The story that you tell about Parabrahman and the Divine Accident and the longing to be One again. Is it also fiction? Is it a mythological story?

K: In the beginning there was no beginning and in the end there'll be no end.

Q: Is this only a fiction?

K: Ramana makes Parabrahman to be like a spider. The spider that doesn't know any spider – a potential of a spider. Then the potential spider wakes up. Then out of a potential, there's a spider, like consciousness spinning whatever – instantly! Then this imaginary spider, the *experience* of a spider, tries to find its nature in this spider web. And at one point maybe it realizes that it cannot catch itself in its own web because it's always so tricky. Who knows the trap? It's really Intelligence itself, it cannot be trapped by Itself. At that moment it says that by whatever understanding I cannot know myself! Then it withdraws the whole web and comes back to the potential. But in the potential, there's no memory of that. So, the moment the spider wakes up again, it starts spinning again, trying to catch itself.

This is an Infinite story. Like Shiva creating the puppet house and now trying to play with the puppets... and by playing with the puppets he forgets that he's not a puppet. Then it starts again. Then being a puppet trying *not* to be a puppet confirms the puppet again! And by accident again the puppet dies. Then it is surprised that 'I'm even *without* the puppet'... and it never needed any puppet. Wow, I'm not even the puppeteer because even *that* is a puppet!

Meditating on death is like... 'nothing ever happened'. It is the only way out... of being That what was never *in*. Killing that idea that you have to *exist* to exist... and by that, being that what doesn't even *need* to exist to exist. All the ideas of life and death are gone, but not by understanding something! You have to face that infinite absence... call it whatever. But this is life and death which is in nature not different. It's here-now – just here. So, meditate! [Laughter]

Q [Another visitor]: What did you do with the fingers...

K: It's a Mudra. It keeps your relative attention to the fingers but That what is that attention goes to that point. It keeps your relative attention occupied. The mind gets occupied just by holding the fingers. [Pointing his arm forward and touching three fingers] This is the Trinity, the father, the spirit and the son. Then you ask why should I do it? I say, just do it because then your hands are occupied and not in your trousers somewhere! [Laughter] You make this position so that your body is quiet, it's like an energy thing. That the energy is not bothering you, that the perception goes to that what is the imaginary point. Then going where nothing is there, it expands into that infinite absence. So, try it and if you come back tell me how it worked.

Q [Another visitor]: Is this same like deep-deep sleep?

K: No because now you're aware about it. Now you want to know what is in deep-deep sleep. But that you can only know by looking at the absence now and not in deep-deep sleep.

Q: Can you be conscious in the absence?

K: You are aware of the trinity... but What-you-are is in spite of it. But in deep-deep sleep you cannot make it the memory of your body, but it seems like in the memory of this system, it doesn't need to be reminded anymore. Then it's not a brain fuck or an intelligent understanding, it's just an experience of absence - and that experience is eating you up because in that experience you cannot remain as a 'me'. But deep-deep sleep remains like a pointer but if 'you' still survive in it, it becomes like an imaginary deep-deep sleep. But this is an *experience* of deep-deep sleep, because no one can remain in that. So, you are in the presence and in the absence of anything. That was my message from the Ashram! [Laughter]

Forty years ago I read a book in German about Buddhist methods of meditation which talked about what is the wisdom of emptiness? The wisdom of emptiness is that there's no one who's wise in it. You cannot remain in that wisdom of emptiness. It kills you, because no 'one' can be there in that absolute absence of any presence. In the presence you can survive but not in the absence. If you want to kill the 'me', you've to meditate or contemplate on the absence because the absence kills you. That's Ramana's stirring the stick in the fire, which is the coolest fire of absence. In the absolute coolness of absence, you cannot remain as a hot man or a hot woman.

Q: What is the difference between suicide and this kind of meditation?

K: Your idea of suicide is killing the body but this is killing the 'me' – the killer. That's quite a difference. So, kill the killer by being the absence, as you are the presence. But it seems like in the presence you always survive as the one who's present. But in the absence you cannot survive as one who's present. So, the absence kills you and not the presence.

[Pointing to a visitor] Is this a good medicine?

Q [Another visitor]: It looks like it...

K: So, try it... but I'll not repeat it again because you make it like a shit factory again, you make something out of it. You try to find a tactic of how to survive in the absence. You already think about it... 'How can I make it work for me?' Of course, it works like that, all the time. [Pointing to a visitor] She already thinks, what can I do? How can I stay there? Maybe I have to become nothing to remain there. That's quite a trick of all masters. I'm nothing... so I can still be someone where there's an absence. So, they make even an absence as a presence where they can survive in. All the things by Robert Adams... 'I'm nothing, you're nothing'. It's just a survival system. Like in nothing you can survive, but not as *something*. 'I'm nothing, I can survive now!' [Laughing] So, it's still not killed!

It's quite a famous technique even for masters to remain as a Master, the one who knows his true nature, to call himself as nothing... 'I'm nothing, you're nothing, we're all nothing!' [Yawning] Nothing is still too much in the absence. There's no nothing in absence. Nothing and everything are in the presence, but not in the absence!

Q [Another visitor]: Is this meditation better than...

K: This is not a meditation. This is a concentration camp. [Laughter]

Q [Another visitor]: So, you're not serious about anybody doing any practice?

K: Exactly. I'm not serious about anybody 'doing' meditation, for sure not. Because if you're there doing meditation, if *you're* meditating – fuck it all, that's not meditation! So, I'm for sure not serious about any meditator. How can you *do* meditation? How can you *exercise* meditation?

Q: So, when you say meditate on that, what are you actually saying?

K: *You* disappear in it! There's meditation without a meditator because you cannot expect anything out of absence. The peace idea is only in the presence. So, you try to meditate on peace so that you get something out of peace...you get more peace of mind or something. But it's all in the presence because the absence never delivers anything! There's no harvesting, there's nothing coming out of harvesting in absence. In that there is no harvester possible. It kills the harvester, it kills your intention of getting something, because the absence doesn't give you anything. But all the other things, world peace and inner peace and that peace, peace off peace! [Laughter] There's always expectation in it. 'I want to have more bliss in meditation'. You meditate for bliss, what kind of meditation is that? A blister meditation!

And you don't have to sit down on cold stones to do this. You can just make your dishes, the absence point is always there. You just look there and make your dishes. [Laughter] You don't have to become a hemorrhoids master being surrounded by angry meditators.

Q [Another visitor]: [Laughing] So, having a straight back is not necessary?

K: No straight back. Just be in the most comfortable position, making dishes or watching television because even while watching television you can be in the absence position. I tell you, this is twenty-four by seven. This is not specially sitting down and having an intention... 'Now I meditate on the absence, especially 'me' meditating now on the absence'. No! It's twenty-four by seven, it's always available, it's always there, it's not something that's not there.

Q [Another visitor]: Papaji used to sit in front of the television and sometimes the television was over but he just sat there...

K: So, he didn't watch television. But *you* watch television! That's why he liked cricket because cricket is boring enough that you can just relax. [Laughter] That's why Indians like cricket so much because you don't have to watch, nothing happens anyway. In India and Australia the most famous meditation is watching cricket. You can be gone and you don't miss anything. It's like listening to your wife, that's the best meditation. But then the tricky questions come... 'How do I look today?' [Laughter] Then you say 'okay'... What? I just look okay today?

Q [Another visitor]: Whatever we do, in the beginning the intention is always there...

K: As Happy-Nappy pointed out, put your attention only to the absence awareness, then the stick will go by itself. Okay, you have to do something in the beginning. What are you doing here? Lazy bastards. [Laughter] You think I do everything for you? [Pointing to a visitor] Look at her, the most lazy bastard from Spain... 'Why should I do these stupid gestures? I better make honey and olive oil at home because I get money out of it. Why should I look at this blankness?' You will be frustrated because nothing comes out of it. And I like that. I like frustrated business men!

The fire for yourself must be so strong that you don't care what you get out of it. The moment you want to get something out of it, you're fucked for a long time after that. That's why Ramana said you have to be ten metres under water and the only way out is being What-you-are and then you may... because there's no interest in the world anymore, in getting something out of it. Then it may work or not... but not by your intention. So, you have to devote yourself absolutely to What-you-are.

Meditating on that absence is destroying whatever can be destroyed and What-you-are will be the leftover and not, 'What would I get out of it?' That what you get out of it is really worth it because the absolute advantage of not needing one is incomparable... and you're longing for that. But now you become a businessman wanting your little peace. Keep your bloody little peace and leave me alone. All these greedy bastards around. 'Give me some technique where I can get something out of it. I want to have some jolly, folly, dolly... [Laughter] And I want to be in peace. What do I get out of it if *I'm* not there when there's peace?' [Laughter] That's the *main* thing – Why should I look for something where I'm not? I still look for something where I can still survive.

Q [Another visitor]: In a way, you confuse me...

K: I hope! [Laughter]

Q: In the beginning, there was this fire in me when I was with Osho...

K: But it didn't work. Did he ever tell you this meditation? It was people jumping around doing dynamic meditation or closing-your-eyes-and-being-quiet meditation. [Laughter] If you really would have that fire in you for that meditation, you would not sit here anymore.

Q: I have the intention...

K: Intention is the worst case scenario for meditation. I want something with all my heart, but it was all too much. You have to be a *cool* fire, no interest anymore, no intention and not this burning heart, wanting something, full of fire. The fire has to be already burnt out and not that 'I'm now full of fire', and all that. Osho tried to burn it down, but it's still burning. [Laughter]

Worthless, worthless, worthless! Futile exercise from Osho. He tried to exhaust something that is inexhaustible. He tried very hard but he always failed.

Q [Another visitor]: So, I relax in that and then?

K: You cannot relax. Then you have intention of relaxation and that's too much because then 'I' relax! And then? And then? And then?... Come on! You can do better. [Mocking] 'Satisfy me so that I believe in you... and if I believe in what you're saying, then maybe I do it'.

Q: I'm confused...

K: I hope you're confused because you *want* something. Greedy bastard, you know that!

Q: So, what to do?

K: Go home and do your homework and come back later. [Laughter] Then they want something from me but I don't give you anything, I tell you. You may be a sucker but I'm not something that you can suck – finished! [Laughing] There are others you can suck... go to Rishikesh. [Laughter] There you get rishis for cash. [Laughter] That's why it's called Rishikesh. Re-lax-man Jhoola yoga, it's very relaxing... 'And I was sitting in the same place as John Lennon. Then I imagine and imagine and imagine All the fucking people!' [Laughter] And the TM, Maha wishy-washy, the laundry of existence. Clarifying the mind by meditating on the TM, transcendental. He was a dentist for the whole world. Now we have Eckhart who wants to heal the world. Where do all these doctors come from? [Laughter]

Q [Another visitor]: Is belonging something personal or is it something resonating from...

K: Belonging is always personal. Belonging comes from a person who is born, then there's longing. The person doesn't want to be a person, then there's longing, so what? Try to long without 'you'! [Laughter] [Whining] I'm so much in longing, I'm so much on fire for myself, it's just horniness. You want to penetrate yourself, you horny bastard who wants to penetrate himself because you want to *know* yourself. 'I want to know myself very deeply, inside out. I want to penetrate whatever can be penetrated in front of me'. God became a dog and now the dog is hot... a hotdog. [Laughter] A hotdog who wants to be one with everything!

I make it drastic but it *is* like that. The moment God knows himself he becomes a dog, and then he's horny to know himself. At first there's a little honeymoon... but I call it a horny moon. Then you penetrate yourself but you get bored by penetrating yourself and then you look for something else.

Q [Another visitor]: Is it true to say that while you need anything from this world, it is...

K: No. The tiger just plays with you and by *accident* it swallows you! But you're already in the tiger's mouth, don't worry. It will eat you but not when you *want* to be eaten. It eats you in spite of you wanting to be eaten. You don't have to be on a barbecue to be ready for the tiger. [Pointing to a visitor] She is a moth who wants to be on a barbecue... hot! [Laughter] I bar-beg-you! Come on, eat me! And the tiger says, 'Why should I kill something that I want to play with?'

Q: When you're quiet does the tiger take you?

K: When the goat is quiet, the tiger has no interest. In a zoo somewhere there's a tiger and a goat living together... no interest. The goat was just not interested in running away so the tiger didn't run after it. Maybe the tiger only runs after someone who's trying to run away? [Laughter] When something is quiet, there's no interest. You want to flock like a goat and that's called Sadhana. Making yourself more attractive for the tiger by being quieter.

Q [Another visitor]: Just trying to attract the tiger...

K: You think the tiger is not fast enough for you?

Q: It's just that the tiger is lazy...

K: It cannot be lazy because the tiger is in front of you and behind of you and on every side and everywhere. How can it be lazy? Just by being everywhere, it kills you anyway. You cannot run away from yourself, come on! This idea that you have to be quiet to be eaten, is quite an idea. But it sounds good... 'I'll be quiet so that the Self can find me more easily'. Ha ha ha! [Laughter] And I must dress in maroon, maybe the bull wants to pierce me then. All these Sannyasi colors, they think if the bull sees red, it follows it. [Laughter]

Q [Another visitor]: That's the traditional teaching...

K: That's called tradition... but if *I* make a traditional teaching, everyone goes over the top! This is traditional too. This is a totally traditional Buddhist advice. This is not something new that I invent.

The good thing is you don't have to sit quietly to do it. You can do it permanently, being whatever. Forget it! I don't say it anymore. Pearls for the swine again.

Q [Another visitor]: You told me to be Absolute and that's my main practice...

K: That makes you the Absolute because it shows you that you *are* the Absolute and are not dependent on any presence, because the Absolute doesn't need a presence to exist. The Absolute is in the *presence* and in the *absence*. But now you believe that you have to know that. But you *know* that you cannot get less by the absence or more by presence. You know that you are in whatever circumstance What-it-is. But you want to *become* it by looking at Arunachala. [Pointing to a visitor] She wants to get it for nothing.

Q [Another visitor]: When I look at Arunachala, can it be similar to disappearing in nothingness?

K: No, because you see a mountain, I tell you. [Laughter] And you look at the mountain because you want to get something out of it, you know that! Everyone who looks at the mountain... 'I'm here, I'm ready, Come on! I came a long way. Now perform, give me something. Come on fire! Come on light! Burn me, I'm ready! But only in January and February'. [Laughter] These are the Arunachala tourists, otherwise she makes honey and olive oil at home to sell something. Then she has a little Arunachala in front of her. Then she comes here to Arunachala... 'Come on baby, I don't have much time!' [Laughter] [Pointing to another visitor] She's here for one week... 'Come on, give it! I'm under pressure, Ayurveda is waiting for me. My Candida is more important than you, come on!' [Laughter]

Everyone is like that in a way. I have some spare time so I look at Arunachala. Okay, for one week I devote all my attention and then you have to deliver now. I devote my precious life, my precious time I give to you... Come on! especially 'me'!... and when it doesn't deliver you say, 'Oh Arunachala is just another mountain'. [Laughter]

The worst thing was, I was for four years in Holland for the Science and Non-duality gatherings. I thought if I don't go maybe I was being arrogant. So, I had to see by myself that I was not arrogant, I just had good intuition! [Laughter] Then there was Unmani who said, 'I was in Arunachala in the last season but I didn't feel anything. I think when you realize your true nature before you come to the mountain, you cannot feel anymore'. Imagine someone saying that! Fantastic! What does it show? I thought, you keep your true nature and leave me alone! 'I' realized 'my' true nature before 'I' went, so 'I' didn't feel anything! Whoah! And now she has a baby.

So, meditate on absence. Un-mani(on money) will not work. It has to be the absence.

Q [Another visitor]: Unmani says, die to Love...

K: Fuck it all. She even says Truth is all in the presence. You'll survive in love, you'll survive in presence, you'll survive in whatever, but not in the absence. My fucking true nature! Especially *'my'* fucking true nature... 'I realized 'my' true nature'. Aww...

So many stories, so many claims. All the claims, the claimer whatever you can have... is all in the presence. Then they say you have to give your total attention to the presence, this 'now'. What is this bloody now? Pressure! Then you're in a pressure cooker and you think you get cooked by the pressure cooker of now. And what comes out? A ready meal? Another hotdog who is ready to be eaten?

Q [Another visitor]: The 'I' which is the ego is not afraid of the absence. The ego is very experienced...

K: But the ego needs experiences to exist. So, it is afraid of the absence because in the absence it cannot exist. By all means it tries to avoid the absence.

Q: But usually the ego is not afraid...

K: Of course it's afraid.

Q: No. When it goes to bed every night.

K: It doesn't go to bed, it's dropped. The ego doesn't fall asleep, the ego gets dropped. You think the ego is in deep-deep sleep?

Q: So it must be an experience...

K: The ego is an experience that gets dropped every night and in the morning it waits for you so that you give attention to it, because without your attention, there's no ego! You drop the ego and in the morning you're stupid enough to pick it up again. [Laughter] That's called a Swiss cuckoo clock... 'I'm here, what took you so long? Eight hours sleep is enough, I was waiting for you'. [Laughter] You think the ego ever sleeps? You think the ego is awake now? What are you dreaming about?

There's no ego now and there's no ego in deep-deep sleep. What is an ego? A fucking idea that no one has ever found. Show me the ego! You can just call me a concept of – whatever. You don't even know what it is. You just repeat what you said or what someone told you. You call that ego, that's all. It's a hearsay.

Q: It's a construct...

K: It's not even a construct because then there would be a construction. But who works in a construction?

Q: Construction-deconstruction...

K: Fuck it all! There's no construct at all. A cluster of energy, that you call ego. What is that? A cluster.

Q: Why are we afraid of death if it's just like deep-deep sleep?

K: Because it's fun... just for fun, you imagine there's a boogie man somewhere. You don't even know if it exists or not. You dance with fear, like a horror movie. And a horror movie without fear doesn't work. So, you have fear but you don't even know for what. Then the movie is over and you go home and drink tea. The whole story of this body is a horror movie. How can you enjoy this horror movie without fear?

The movie becomes such a good movie because everything including fear is there. It's such an exciting movie because there's a fear that maybe I can die. I'm so excited that I can die, maybe something can happen. Maybe I get sick, wow! Maybe I should eat healthy or maybe I die by eating healthy, let's see! Where's the ego?

Q: It's a bubble...

K: I can't even call it anything. It's just an imaginary... you don't even know what it is.

Q: One morning, I woke up from deep sleep and somehow there was no ego...

K: No! And then?

Q: It was a great feeling...

K: Like Susan Segal. Have you read her book? She lost her ego in Paris on a bus stand. Then she went to all the masters to find out what was wrong. She had this fear that something was wrong with her because she doesn't have this ego experience anymore. It's like you lose your centre or a reference point in a way. There's an imaginary reference point to look from. You just pick-up an imaginary camera position. She lost that and she was full of fear.

Then suddenly she claimed that... 'Now it's all love. There was a little fear but now it's an ocean of love and there's a little plant of fear. It's so little that you don't even mention it. It's just something. I don't see it anymore, but it's there. But there's this ocean of love!' Two years later out of this little plant of fear came an ocean of fear and then she died by cancer. For some time there was a love experience but she was not killed in it. So, whatever experience you have, this love, this blissful thing, it comes back. And this little fear, this little plant grows up to a big tree and there's an ocean of fear again.

How to out root that little plant? What is the only way of out rooting this – whatever? You think you can kill it by love? You only make it grow even bigger. The only way of out rooting the idea that 'you' exist is that you meditate on the absence of existence and by experiencing the absolute absence of existence, you're not dependent on a presence. That's killing the fear. You are in the death experience That which you are in the life experience, and nothing can make you more or less as you are, where is the fear?

Q: But how can you work like this?

K: This is not a practice, this is not a process, this is not an evolutionary – whatever. This is just confronting yourself with death permanently, twenty four hours a day, three sixty-five days meditating on the absence. And maybe then... okay! Then for a few times you'll expand into eternity and come back. You open up and you close. It opens up and it closes again, so, get used to it. You're in the openness What-you-are and in the closeness What-you-are. Then you relax in it.

Then by whatever awareness that nothing can make you more as you are, you burn out that idea that something can happen to you. Now there's this energy of fear, a fear of dying, a fear of consequence. But even in the absence there's no consequence for you, and nothing has a consequence for What-you-are. So, whatever you experience has no consequence. You're in spite of all happenings and non-happenings What-you-are! In the total absence of any consequence... where's the fear?

So, if you ask me first you have to make a little effort to give your attention to the absence, not because it makes you What-you-are but because you fear the absence. But you have to confront it because that's the only thing that's sure - that you die! This will be gone. Everything else is a fiction anyway. There's maybe one thing that you cannot avoid is that this thing will be gone one day and you have to be without it. So, why not now being with and without it? Then this body can do whatever, it can become whatever. Who cares when it dies?

That's Ramana. He really didn't care, it can take another twenty years. Who cares? It will be gone one day so it's already gone. And you're still What-you-are in the absence of it! That is this death experience of Ramana that you can read in the Ashram. But before that he claimed that one year earlier Arunachala came into him like an energy and by that energy he burnt. It's like a fire of the Heart and then he confronted that and in one thing, he was gone. But who knows how many lifetimes before he had to burn these tendencies. He said himself, who knows how many lifetimes he has meditated before. People would always ask him, you never meditated and this happened to you and he said who knows how many life times I had to do things before this one? Who knows? Everything is possible.

Q: It's all by Grace?

K: It depends on how many lifetimes it takes for these tendencies to burn out. Maybe it takes a long long time. But it will burn out. You can trust, but before that all whatever you do is a concept.

It's *already* grace working here... there's nothing but grace working here. So, what to do? Trust yourself because *you're* grace and without grace you could not even exist, you could not breathe, there would be nothing. There's everything because of grace and there's nothing because of grace. So, *be* the Grace... *be* the Reality realizing itself! And how to be the Reality realizing itself? How to do that?

Only in the fearlessness of your existence, you're That. Then the snake becomes the rope again, that's all! This... whatever you experience in this presence cannot make you more or less as you are! So, what can happen to you? All what you experience has no consequence for your nature – never had, never will have! This was the first question today – What is the consequence? Fearing the consequence, that is fearing death. But there's no consequence and that's the death of the ego because the ego – the imaginary one – exists from consequences. How can there be fear without consequences? Tell me!

And what makes you to hang on to all these little things? Love! Fuck love, I tell you and be What-you-are. And the love for your Self doesn't come from any 'one'. The love for the Self means killing everything! It's killing the lover and the beloved just by being that What-it-is. The devotion is the devotion of the Self. It is giving up all the ideas of What-it-is and What-it-is-not and only you, the Self, can give up the *idea* of self and no one else can do it for you.

Q [Another visitor]: Yesterday you said you realize yourself in the presence and you realize yourself in the absence...

K: No. The Self is realizing Itself in the presence and in the absence... but That what is realizing Itself in the presence and the absence cannot be realized.

Q: You mentioned that the Self realizes itself in Awareness as one...

K: Yes... That's the beginning of the realizer. The Awareness is the realizer realizing itself in presence and absence. But the realizer is not that What-you-are. You're the Nature of the realizer which is *with* and *without* the realizer. The Awareness would be the Father, the Holy Spirit is the absence and the Presence is the Man, or Jesus. That what *is* the Father – the Creator, the realizer – is realizing itself in the absence and in the presence. But What-you-are is not the realizer. You are the *Heart* of the Realizer, the absence and the presence. You are the Heart of all of that. This is the trinity of Shiva and you're the Heart of that. You're Shiva realizing itself in the absence and the presence.

Q: But what I am is something...

K: Beyond your imagination.

Q: So, I can't be realized?

K: No.

Q: So, how can we talk about it?

K: Look at me! Listen to me and then you'll see how can we talk about it – just listen!

Q: But it can't be realized...

K: But look... I *talk* about it!

Q: It can't be experienced...

K: It cannot *not* be experienced! The Absolute experience that you are... *that* you cannot get rid of! The Absolute experience that you are, which is without an experiencer, which is Heart *being* Heart, not needing an experience of heart. Without that Absolute experience that you are, there's no experiencer, and no experiencing whatever can be experienced!

Without the Absolute experience that you are – the Absolute being – there's no possibility of any *experience* of being. But prior to the experience of one who is, is that what is Heart, which is your Nature or Silence, call it whatever. I would not call it anything. Just be That what is in spite of anything!

So, don't try to imagine that what is imagining everything because That what is imagining everything can never be part of the imagination. So, whatever you can imagine or non-imagine, because imagining is presence and non-imagining is absence. Even the non-imagination is still an imagination! So, even the absence is an imaginary absence and the presence is an imaginary presence. But What-you-are is not. And that you will never know! You can never add a quality or an attribute to it. Anything that you say about it doesn't work. It only works for the one who claims that he realized his true nature. Then he can become a teacher, then he can share something what he has. But That what is your nature can never be shared. You can never share What-you-are, not even with yourself. Otherwise you become a sheep shearer, you become a shepherd again. Then you want to 'share' the sheep.

[A Visitor moves out]

You see, when it has to happen, you have to go to the toilet.

Q: In your previous talk you spoke about who knows how many lifetimes that Ramana had to practice before. What is the purpose of speculating about the previous lives of what might have been or not have been?

K: It's good entertainment… it's just pointers! By Grace alone things happen and not by your effort. You can only make an effort because Grace allows you to do that and not by you. It's just a pointer that in his lifetime it was just Grace and not him who did it. Grace just blindly took him. It's always blind. The Heart is blind, it has no eyes.

Q: Perhaps he was willing to be taken?

K: No, even that doesn't work! In *spite* of being willing or not willing, he was taken and not *because*… in *spite* of one who was being quiet. Maybe it happens even then, but not because.

Q: Maybe Ramana was a young child and children are more open…

K: Whatever you try to make it as a circumstance, doesn't work! That what is the Self doesn't need any special circumstance at all. It's always in *spite* of any circumstance of readiness or ripeness. It doesn't know any readiness or ripeness for anyone… it's just blind!

Q: It's just blind luck?

K: There's not even luck involved! If it's meant to happen, it will happen. But not because you want it. If it's meant to happen, it will happen in spite of your effort, in spite of what you've done, in spite of all the sadhanas, in spite of whatever.

Q: In spite of coming here?

K. For sure in spite of coming here! That I always say, you will not become What-you-are by listening to me. But it may not harm either! [Laughter]

Most people coming here have some experience and they're not able to place it anywhere. So, we can talk about what it is.

Q: And talking about it is just chatter?

K: It's just sport… it's not making or unmaking anything. It's not an advantage at all. It's more like cricket… this is cricket talk!

Q [Another visitor]: I'm realizing myself as a person and now you say go to the impersonal experience?

K: No, I didn't say that. The impersonal is impersonal and the personal is personal, it's not the same, they're different.

Q: The impersonal 'I Am' is just an idea...

K: Yes and I tell you it's not the 'I Am'. The 'I Am' is part of the presence. The 'I Am' is still personal. There's a personal 'I am the body', there's a personal 'I Am' and a personal 'I' – that's the *presence*. Then the other side is the *absence* which is impersonal 'I', the impersonal 'I Am' and the impersonal world. These are the personal and the impersonal and you are the zero-zero. You're That what doesn't get personal in the personal and not impersonal in the impersonal. You're not *personal* in the personal experience and you're not *impersonal* in the impersonal experience. You're That what is realizing itself in personal and the impersonal. But the personal doesn't make you personal *and* the impersonal doesn't make you impersonal. The presence doesn't make you present and the absence doesn't make you absent. You are always that What-you-are.

That's what they call the omni-presence or the omni-*pre*-sense of What-you-are! And that you cannot imagine, that you can only *be*.

Q: Even the idea of it already feels good...

K: Then stay there... but it's not meant to feel good. I am not here to provide blissful experiences – absolutely not! I am not here to give any bliss. But maybe you can still have some... I can be very generous.

No, this is not a wellness... whatever. I'm not here for wellness, this is not about wellness or well-being... not at all! This is not about chanting or singing Bhajans or anything that makes you feel better or at least I hope so! [Laughter] But if you feel better, it's okay as well. Shit happens! [Laughter]

Q [Another visitor]: What is reacting to this provoking?

K: It doesn't matter. That what is reacting to this provoking is not What-you-are.

[Pointing to the visitor] Looking at his smiling face, you'd never know there's something behind. It's fantastic! I always like the Buddha figures with a smile and now everyone in the West has these Buddha figures in every garden. Then you think you have to look like Buddha to be Buddha. I like these grumpy bastards sitting around giving a shit about how they look. Maybe that's more the Buddha face. [Groaning] [Laughter]

Buddha doesn't have to show that he's a Buddha and that one who needs to show that he's a Buddha is for sure not Buddha. Would Buddha claim that he has realized his true nature? Tell me. Would he say things like that? There's a hearsay that he said, 'I always failed. I failed to know myself, I even failed not to know myself. I failed absolutely. In whatever I tried to do, I failed'. By that he is that what he is. You can call it the Buddha but Buddha would never call himself a Buddha.

In that sense... fail!

Q [Another visitor]: About 'Be what you are'...

K: I would call it be what you cannot *not* be. This koan creates a little gap in your brain.

Q: It seems to be the same for everybody...

K: There's no everybody in that... that's the nature of life.

Q: Does it mean Oneness?

K: No. You can say Oneness is absence. In absence there's oneness because there's an absence of separation. In absence there's oneness and in presence there's separation and both come together. But when there's oneness there's separation, or twoness... twoness and oneness come together, but you're neither! The experience of twoness doesn't make you separate and the experience of oneness doesn't make you one. You're neither one nor two. So *neti-neti*... that's the main thing, neither that *nor* that!

Q: So what are you left with?

K: You are the Absolute leftover which is left with that what he is... neither knowing nor not knowing it... That which is the Absolute leftover who cannot *not* be. So, this will take a while. You are that what you call Reality or Self and you have to realize yourself, in separation or oneness... in all possibilities. In all possibilities of presence and all impossibilities of absence, you have to realize yourself in all of that. And you cannot get rid of yourself. There's no way out of you being What-you-are and by being What-you-are, you have to realize yourself!

It's not like you are a person who has to realize his true nature and there's a way out. No! You are That which has no way in and no way out! You are That and this is What-you-are. This beingness and non-beingness is What-you-are! You're in being and in not-being That what can never *not* be what it is!

Q [Another visitor]: Is the personal 'I' a product of the conditioning of the mind?

K: It's a product of this body. It's a product of this cluster of energy that's built up as a body that creates a centre. The body is a genetic design of the past that now creates an ego or a 'me' as a centre of it... but it's as imaginary as the body. It *comes* with the body and it *goes* with the body! The last words of Nisargadatta when he died was, 'Now with this body, the so-called traces of Nisargadatta are leaving me'.

Q: It begins as a three year old...

K: No. It was already there before. The genetic condition happens much before that. Your father and mother giving all that addition. The ego was already there a long time ago.

Q: It only happens when you're a baby...

K: With the 'I', the centre gets created but the conditioning was already there. Then the cluster gets a centre but the centre is different every day.

Q: What if we did not condition the baby?

K: Try it! People have tried it and it didn't work. The moment there was a particular circumstance, the centre appeared. The conditioning was already there before the baby was there. The ancestors of all the happenings before created the information of that body and everything is already there. Then the 'I' is just a centre where you look from. It's just a camera position that you call as ego, a reference point, that's all. But the reference point changes permanently, so it cannot even be fixed somewhere.

Q: It's like a coordinating point?

K: It's a coordinating point, like a reference where you speak from, where you look from. It's like an imaginary centre where you act from. But it's changing permanently, every day someone else wakes up. You cannot find anything stable about it. It's permanently changing and shifting and doing things. You really have to make a lot of effort to memorize what happened before and how you are, because if you don't memorize how you are, there's no 'me' anymore! Every morning you have to jump in, memorizing how you are and how you react to a circumstance otherwise you don't exist. It's just a little memory effect, like a computer memory. Then there's a software program running, trying to keep things in check. Trying to make it a good ego. A lifetime work of being a good person!

And some really succeed, that's the worst case scenario, if there's really a good person coming out or something! Then he becomes a role model for everyone and everyone feels bad around this good person. [Laughter] They're the worst case scenario! If you find a good person, you should just run right away! [Laughter] Bad persons make everyone happy because everyone feels better than that one. [Laughter] So, whenever you meet a good person, shoot him... it's a good deed. [Laughter] Especially if he *claims* to be good, that's the worst case scenario.

Q [Another visitor]: Even in Nisargadatta's case, right up to his death, he was speaking from a reference point...

K: As long as there's a body, you talk from something... but what's the problem? Sometimes you talk from a little Karl, from a dirty mind, sometimes you talk from the holy spirit. What's the problem? You have a rainbow spectrum of being really bad and being the holiest. Why do you limit yourself to this little shade of 'me'? Just be the biggest bastard and the biggest saint of all time because What-you-are, you are that anyway. You're the lowest and the highest but you're not low when you're low and when you're not high you're high. You can be the most stupid and ignorant that you cannot imagine and you still are What-you-are. Isn't that amazing? You don't have to be a clever bastard who knows all the tricks, who knows how to speak and how to behave so that people believe that you got something that they don't have. [Speaking meekly] 'I love you'... [Groaning] Ho, ho, ha, ha... [Laughter]

Q [Another visitor]: So the clever ones have no chance?

K: Even the *not* clever ones have no chance! Don't make it like you have to become an idiot to become What-you-are! [Laughter] I know many people believe in that – 'Now I have to become an idiot, an ignorant one and then I will become what I am'.

Q: I want to try that...

K: It's fun... trying to become an idiot, that's very clever! [Laughter] You must be very clever to play an idiot. Good luck!

Any other questions?

Q [Another visitor]: You killed us all...

K: The ducks will pop-up again the moment I'm gone, you know that.

Q: Unfortunately, yes...

K: No... *fortunately* yes... otherwise I have nothing to shoot anymore! [Laughter] This is a fair where you have a shooting game filled with ducks. You shoot, shoot, shoot and then in the back they start popping up again. They come back as same, fresh ducks. And the duck knows that you can shoot me but I'll come back. [Laughter] They're all like Schwarzenegger – *hasta la vista* baby, I'll be back. [Laughter]

It's like when you get enlightened, you shot all the ducks. But the moment you relax, they're all back. [Laughter] Nice try! Especially the one who believes that he destroyed his ego – 'I killed my ego'! [Laughter]

Q [Another visitor]: Kalashnikov... [Laughter]

K: It's all a *karasho* [Very good]. In Moscow I said it's all a horror show and everyone understood as *karasho*. [Laughter] The moment you say something, there's a misunderstanding. It's *all* a horror show, even Osho. One there was O-sho, now there's no-show. [Laughter]

Q [Another visitor]: Why is it so difficult to confront ugliness in the presence?

K: You mean when you look in the mirror? I'm so bad! [Laughter]

What do you mean by ugliness? Show me any ugliness and you just show me beauty.

Q: There's some kind of feeling of disgust...

K: You have some ugliness inside which you'd like to vomit out? Okay, try! Vomit the ugliness and then beauty remains. You create an absence and that's beauty? Don't eat anymore... can you do that? Then you'd have to eat Prana. [Pointing to a visitor] She wanted to export this therapy to India. I think she should go to America, they waste more food than India can ever eat.

I like all those ideas – eating Prana... as if there's anything else to eat! What else can you eat? What else can you eat as divine food? What is *not* divine? Come on! Even the cunt of a bitch is divine. That was the most famous pointer by Ramakrishna. Even the cunt of a bitch has as much divinity, and now I add – as the balls of the Pope. Divine father with his divine balls. [Laughter] He became pope only because now he can wear Italian shoes. Argentineans believe that they're Italians from South America. [Laughter]

Q [Another visitor]: You said something about being a good person. Can you say something more about it?

K: It's an idea... a good person can only be good because some other person is ugly or nasty. Who creates the good one and who creates the nasty one? It needs a concept of good and a concept of bad; both need each other. A good person needs a bad person and a bad person needs a good person to exist.

Q: Is there genuinely any good hearted person?

K: It's an idea. A person has no heart, it's just a pumping system. Could you find your heart?

Q: It's the feeling of goodness inside...

K: Those are good feelings. Then what about the bad feelings? You need to define that good feelings are one way and bad feelings are another way. You need an idea about good and bad, about what feels good and what feels bad. You need a reference point of good and bad. You need a concept of something. You need a concept of humanity so that one person needs to be good to another person, so that a good person doesn't kill another person or doesn't rip-off someone. In other societies it may be the opposite, you never know.

When I came here earlier in India you would be imprisoned for abortion. Then a few years later, you got ten thousand rupees for abortion. The person who was once a bad person, two years later he got a medal for it. So, what is good and what is bad? It's just an agreement between people of whatever fits. It needs some reference and a need of the moment. In that sense, what is good?

Q: So, an offering is not necessary?

K: Be as you are – that's all! You don't need to have any concept that you need to be good or anything, just be as you are. Because Life is living you as Life is living you and Life has no standard of good or bad. The life you are, is now living you as that. That's life living and there's no good or bad in it. It's just the way you realize yourself or you live yourself and there's no consequence for What-you-are in it. Just be that what is living itself, and that's goodness itself! That's the nature of goodness, that doesn't know any goodness. That's why they say God in its nature is good but it's realizing itself in two different ways. So that there can be an experience of good, there has to be an experience of bad. It's realizing itself in good and bad. But the nature of good is good and the nature of bad is good.

That's the same with peace. The nature of God is peace. Shanti is realizing itself in two ways, in relative peace and in relative war. But the nature of peace is Peace and the nature of war is Peace... there's only peace! So, Shanti, Shanti, Shanti... it's not like Shanti, Shanti, war! *Be* the goodness but don't know the goodness... and the goodness doesn't need to be good to be good. And that what needs to be *good* to be good, is what? An idea. It's a prison, an imprisonment of trying to be good or trying to be free. So, be the freedom that doesn't need to be free. And the freedom you want to have, is imprisonment... it's a prison, it's an idea. Be the freedom that's free from the *idea* of freedom. That's not what you can achieve by anything! You cannot *become* the goodness itself by being good. You can be good or bad, you are anyway What-you-are – never because.

Be the love you are, but the love doesn't know any love. And for that loving, there can be loving or hating, because the nature of hating is as much love as loving. In nature there's no difference. There's unconditional loving and there's unconditional hating. The unconditional love is realizing itself in unconditional love and unconditional hate. You call it hate but don't call it anything. There are differences but it doesn't make you different! It doesn't have to be only one way... *this* comes from heart, and *that* comes from mind, making all those standards! This is a heart person and that's a mind person. The heart blaming the mind and complaining, 'You're talking from the mind and I'm talking from the heart'. Ha ha ha!

That's where all the wars come from, making differences. My way is the right way, my God is the biggest, my God is true, your God is whatever. If any religion says my God is the Almighty, why do they have to fight for Him? Tell me! You only fight for a little bastard God who wants you to fight for him. That's the same with gurus, if you need to fight for your guru and defend him it's for sure not a good one. [Pointing to a visitor] Osho? I poke many here and the moment you defend your guru, you make him small. If he's really your guru, you don't have to defend him at all. If you really have faith in that guru, there's no need to defend him. Only because you don't have faith in him, you defend him. If you really love your guru, you don't have to defend him... only when you're not sure about him, then you defend him.

Now, I'm making standards too. Ha ha ha! [Laughter]

Q [Another visitor]: How to get in tune with Virupaksha cave?

K: The moment you want to be in tune, you're not, because there's one-too-many who wants to be in tune. You're greedy. I know it... all the doctors are greedy. They want to be in tune. With what? You have to get lost in that cave and then the radio Virupaksha is already playing... but to no one!

It's amazing! The moment you want to be in tune, you're cut off because you make two out of it... like 'you' wanting to be in tune with something else. It doesn't work! *Be* the sound, be the *Om* and don't 'try' to be in tune with the primal sound. How to get in tune with Light? By *being* Light and not by being in *tune* with light! It's like first time you go to a brothel and ask, 'How do I get in tune with the whore?' Just have enough money, she'll be in tune with you. [Laughter] At least she'll fake it! If you can't make it, fake it! But you can only fake it sometimes and not all the time, you know that. People say, 'I'm so in tune with the Existence'. It's like a position, 'I'm in tune, my antenna is totally in tune with Existence. I'm the perceiver who's totally in tune with the transmitter'. It's called light and sound meditation... very famous, to get in tune with the light of Shiva. Everyone falls asleep in that.

So, how to stay awake being in that tune? Because when you're in tune, you're asleep... every night the same problem! The moment you're in tune with existence, you fall asleep. Then every morning you wake up because there's a disturbance, because you have to go to toilet or something. The moment you're *not* in tune, you wake up. But then you want to be in tune again... and you've to work your arse off to be in tune again. You have to be tired enough. [Laughter]

So, go to Skandashram... then you go up and down the mountain twice! And if you still have energy, you go again. [Laughter] Then when you totally don't know who you are and who you are not, go to Virupaksha cave and maybe you're in tune... [Laughter] and not like going from the rickshaw to the closest spot! [Laughter]

Q: I'll end up in a hospital rather than Virupaksha cave... [Laughter]

K: Normally they take a rickshaw or taxi to the closest spot and take a short cut. They're full of energy because they want to be in tune. Then they meditate... 'Come on! I'm ready. I had a good breakfast, ten idlies. [Laughter] I'm in my best years of my life. Come on! I'm ready for you to be in tune'.

No! You have to go totally fucked up and exhausted... totally fed up with life. Not dressed like you – at least. (pointing to someone) [Laughter] Not with the golden glasses and things. No, that's why the sadhus they exercise being totally fucked and fed up. But now they all make a business out of it... it doesn't work this way.

Q [Another visitor]: Why is it better to go to Virupaksha cave? Isn't it better to stay in the moment? [Laughter]

K: Why are you here anyway? Why didn't you stay in Denmark? [Laughter] I know it! Because it's too fucking cold and raining there. So, this is called spiritual tourism... you have to be here even in spite of not wanting to be here! That's the main point.

Q: Is it better?

K: Yeah, it is better to be there where you don't want to be. [Laughter] I mean it! The moment you feel well where you are and it's all fine, it's not Sadhana! [Laughter] That's a wellness course or something. Sadhana is being in a place, not wanting to be there. Then experiencing the helplessness that you have no choice in being there where even you don't want to be. That's called the exercise of helplessness... that you cannot decide how you realize yourself. That you, in spite of not wanting to be there where you are, you have to be there. And not like your little decisions – I live in my room, make myself comfortable, make myself chai, then I contemplate. I make everything nice. The laundry lady comes and does my laundry. In the meanwhile I meditate while the roof is being cleaned and the garden is being watered. But I meditate. [Laughter] It's boring but I heard it helps. They say I look better afterwards. [Laughter] People always tell me that I have much less wrinkles when I meditate. I'm more peaceful, I don't kick everyone's arse. So, I stay at home. Sounds good! It's called a yoga class.

Everyone goes to yoga to get a better body. Then they think that now when I have a better body, then I'm ready to meditate. But meanwhile you're old and your body is fucked anyway. If everything is ready and you don't feel your body and everything is healthy, what comes then? Me. Does it work?

[Pointing to a visitor] She's a wellness and health consultant. There'll be a seminar this week – How to get healthy, wealthy and not fucked up. [Laughing]

Thank you and I hope I never see you again... so, you may come but without 'you'.

12th Feb 2016
Tiruvannamalai

Chapter Three

The Peace You Experience, Is Not The Peace You Are

K: I know all the statistics about Valentine's day. Most of the killings happen during Christmas and Valentine. Today is the day of complaints... 'You didn't give what I expected. My whole life is fucked because of you. I chose the wrong one, the neighbour was much better'. [Laughter] The only good movie about Valentine's day was about a shooting and massacre. Let's see what we can do here. [Laughter]

Q: Kill me now... [Laughter]

K: The window is open, whoever wants to jump is welcome. Why should I do the hard work here? [Laughter] If your tendency is bye-bye, then bye-bye! Anyone else who has a suicide tendency and is too afraid to do it himself? [Laughter]

Okay, questions now. Is there love on Earth? [Laughter]

Q: What is this armour around yourself?

K: You're in love with yourself, so you create an armour around you. You want to defend yourself. You're in love with your body and then you create an armour as a defence system, out of love. The love creates the defence system... shit happens! Then you want to open your heart, you want to open your armour, you want to be one with everything. Then once you open your heart, you get everything in and then you complain again... 'That was too much!' It's never right. Anyone who opened his heart here?

[One visitor acknowledges]

K: And how is it?

Q: Painful...

K: Yeah, you have to *pay* for an open heart, especially if you *have* one. So, it's not so pleasant sometimes.

Q: But I don't mind...

K: Because you cannot help it anyway. Now if you want to close it, it becomes even *more* open... it's too late.

Q [Another visitor]: It's really shit...

K: After three kids? You had an open-heart surgery, I see it...

Q: It's closed and it's still too much. It's not bleeding, it's closed... and there's even a scar over it. There's so much fear! Can you tell me about it?

K: I'm very happy that I have no heart. [Laughter] People think they offend me by saying, 'Karl has no heart'. Yes, I agree. [Laughter] What can I do? I'm much too lazy to have a heart. It would be really too hard I know. Having a heart(hard) is really hard!

Q: Is it because of having a heart we are here?

K: Yeah. It's called the heart knot... having a heart and thinking that it needs to be different or something has to be open or closed... and defending your heart and defining what is heart, what is not heart. Boy, it's very very heavy... having a heart is the biggest shit you can have. Shit happens!

Anyone else who has a heart?

Q [Another visitor]: Is it necessary, this armour?

K: If you have a heart, it's necessary! If you have no heart, you don't have to defend anything... it's quite easy. Having a heart – defence, war, you fight for love. Having no heart... what to fight for?

Q: But you cannot help defending...

K: Because you still have a heart.... so defend it!

Q: Even when I don't want to defend, I cannot help. Even not *wanting* to defend...

K: ...is defending your heart. Not defending is another way of defending... so what? Defend your heart, enjoy your ride.

Q: But it's not fun...

K: For me it's fun to look at you. So, if you ask *me*, it's fun!

Q: It's like totally being in love and everything is taken away and you're totally rejected all the time. It's incredible...

K: Sounds like fun. [Laughter] It's volunteering day...

Q: I didn't volunteer for that!

K: You said, take 'me', of course you did! Take me first.

Q: Now even my guru doesn't care to fuck me...

K: What? [Laughter] Even Mad-hooker(Madhukar) doesn't take her any more.

Q: Does he come here?

K: He comes everywhere... why not here? That's his second spiritual name, coming everywhere! [Laughter]

Q: I'm happy that you can have fun with it...

K: What can I do? It's funny! When I see someone who claims to have a heart, it's really funny. It's a joke! Why should I not start laughing? Believing that you have something and fearing to lose it is a joke... so, it's fun! Otherwise she wants me to pity her, show a little bit of compassion. No! I don't show compassion. I *am* compassion and compassion doesn't need anything. I don't have to show off my bloody compassion. The compassion you can show is pity and I don't pity myself in anyway. And if you're in self-pity, it's fun for you and for me too.

Q [Another visitor]: So, there's no action in your compassion?

K: It's silence... Compassion is experiencing yourself in everything. Why should I have pity with compassion? You think you have compassion and now you're in this self-pity idea – Poor me, I have a heart, I exist, what shall I do? [Laughter] [Whining] 'I'm a woman'... [Laughter] Worst case scenario – being a woman and having a heart and finding no man with a heart. So, what to do?

Q [Another visitor]: In France they talk a lot about heart...

K: You can only talk about what you don't have. When you talk a lot about heart, you don't have one. It's like men talk a lot about intellect. [Laughter] Women talk about emotions because they miss them all the time. Men don't have to talk about emotions because they're so fucking emotional. Today we're talking about the heart we don't have – thank God. And I tell you be happy that you don't have a heart. Come on!

Happy-Nappy said when the mind drops, the heart drops along with it. When the mind drops, the owner drops and you remain as That – whatever it is.

Q [Another visitor]: So, Ramana doesn't have a heart?

K: No... his heart went down. If you would have asked Ramana he would have said that it's another idea... having or not having a heart is one owner too many. What to do with that imaginary owner with an imaginary heart? It's false... the idea of heart is for sure false! And *having* a heart is for sure, false! What to do with the falsity? A phantom has a phantom heart. What can one do with a phantom heart? Trying to get rid of it is too much! How to get rid of it? Every morning there's a phantom waking up having a phantom heart... then I say have fun with it because it's a fun-tom!

Not having fun is even more funny. Enjoy yourself as That what you are, because the phantom who tries to have or not have heart will always fight for his bloody heart! This relative love affair will always occupy him... always trying to get advantage from his action or non-action. By having a heart, he tries to have an advantage and by having *no* heart he's just trying another advantage. So, what to do with it?

It's an uninvited guest... and you cannot get rid of this uninvited guest because it doesn't even exist! The more you want to get rid of it, you make it real, that's all! So, whatever you do or don't do wouldn't work. You fail to get rid of that uninvited guest every morning. You can just say, 'One day more'... until the guest is gone anyway. It *came* by itself and it will be *gone* by itself... and you still will be What-you-are... in spite of the guest having or not having, being or not being. It lives only through you. You don't need him but you cannot get rid of him!

So, just let him be because that kills him! You cannot kill him otherwise, you can only kill him by being What you are. There was never any phantom and your nature doesn't depend on any presence or absence of a phantom... that's all! That what *is* Heart doesn't need any idea of heart. You may call yourself That what is Heart... but there is no *owner* of Heart. That's the Kingdom of Heart. But when you're a king who is having a heart, you're king doomed... doomed by being a king of a false heart. The false king having a false heart, that's king doomed and not a king-dom! It's actually king dumb and kingdom.

Q [Another visitor]: I could say the same about the mind...

K: Mind is ownership. You can do this with the whole Consciousness, with whatever you can imagine. It is uninvited, it's an accident! All of that is an accident, you don't need it but it just happened... and now it's too late. How to get rid of this? You didn't want it in the first place and you still don't want it. Now, by accepting something you want to control it. There's no way of accepting that falsity.

You'll never accept that falsity. It will be a false acceptance anyway. And That what you are doesn't need to accept anything because it doesn't even know if there's a world or not!

Q: This morning I was thinking about the golden and the silver and the rainbow. It seems like neither one has any clue about the other two...

K: They all come together! It's the experience of all time. When you experience pure Awareness, the golden honey presence, like the sun. Then the silver is like the moon and it's the presence. And then the rainbow is this world with all its colors and vibrations.

Q: So, why do you say that in the golden you cannot have any experience...

K: You experience the golden Awareness in the presence... like OM. That's why OM is always golden. But the diamond in the middle is not that.

Q: And you're saying that 'you' experience that?

K: Yes. You as the Absolute Seer! That's why Ramana said, only You as the Absolute seer is real and not that what can be seen. But the seer you can see is already false. The Absolute Seer, you can never see. The Absolute Seer experiencing the purest experience or notion of Awareness is golden honey light. That's the first and the last you can experience... then starts your so-called realization. But that what is realizing itself in awareness is not Awareness, it is only *experiencing* itself as awareness. Then comes 'I Amness' which is the spirit and then comes this rainbow... tra la la.

Q: I can't seem to get it...

K: I shift between all of that, sometimes personal, sometimes impersonal; and it doesn't matter. So what? That what I am cannot gain or lose anything by what can be seen. It's always different. The experience of golden awareness is not better than the experience of the rainbow world. They're just different vibrations but they don't *make* a difference, So, what to do?

The best thing is that I really love that I don't have to love anything! I enjoy that I don't have to enjoy anything to be what I am. This joy of being What-you-are, which is in *spite* of whatever you can imagine... is incomparable to all the bloody joy of the rainbow, spirit or golden awareness! All of that is empty for what you are... because it cannot make you more or less as you are. So, enjoy the emptiness of all experiences.

Q: In that sense you can love everything that happens...

K: Why should I love it? That is still *one* relative lover *too many*.

Q: But how does it make a difference for what-is?

K: For me it makes a difference.

Q: But what about Happy-Nappy? Happy-Nappy is Heart and he can swallow whatever he sees...

K: For the Heart there's nothing to swallow.

Q: In love, there's nothing to swallow as well...

K: You *are* the awareness, you *are* the spirit and you *are* the world... so, there's nothing to swallow! You're already That and there's nothing to swallow. What is there to swallow?

Q: What happens from the false...

K: For the Heart, there's no false. But for what you are, That what is *not* false, you have to see the false as false. [Phone rings] [Laughter]

If I have to put it more accurately, if I love it or not, it makes no difference, that's all.

Q: Then why not love?

K: Why not *not* love?

Q: Why *not* love?

K: Love it if you like it. I have no fucking idea of what is right or wrong. So, love it if you love it and don't love it if you don't love it. It's all wrong anyway. [Laughter]

Q: Or all right?

K: All right is too much because than you hang your heart on all right. It doesn't work! All wrong is fine, because wrong is easy to drop. But all fine is heavy – [*speaking in a heavy voice*] 'It's all fine today'. For all wrong, you don't have to do anything, when you wake up it's wrong anyway! Waking up is wrong, and from wrong waking up, wrongness happens! [Laughter] And now you want to make it right... it's too much work!

Q: I just say the opposite of a great truth also has to be a great truth...

K: There's no great truth. Fuck truth and be what you are. Drop this fucking idea of truth. Who needs this fucking truth to be? Say it... 'me'.

Q: It is not 'me'...

K: It is a 'me'! Only when there's a 'me', there's truth. When there's no 'me', there's no truth.

Q: You said, What is, is Heart...

K: I can call it underwear too, I wouldn't mind because that what I am doesn't mind to be called anything. It doesn't need a special word. Calling it Heart is even too much.

Q: It cannot help being Itself...

K: It cannot *not* be what it is, that's all. But it can never *name* itself. It will never call itself Heart.

Q: *You* can call it underwear, but I cannot...

K: I can even call it a piece of shit and I would still not be offended because you cannot offend that what has no sense of being offended. There's no-one who can be offended! So, I can call it a piece of shit and it never minds... because there's no-one who minds in That what you are, I mean it! That's why I like Arunachala! You can call it a piece of shit and Arunachala doesn't mind. [Laughter]

I like this carelessness and not caring about loving or not loving. It's all too late. This 'why' comes from 'me' and there's only one answer... 'Why not'! But for what you are, there's no remedy. There's no medicine to anything. It is always That what is never sick. But this love for yourself makes you sick... and now you became a seeker because your love for yourself became sour. It's a sick love... that's a nice Bob Dylan song. I became a seeker because I'm so love-sick and I keep the love for myself because circumstances are getting worse. [Laughing]

There's always a limit. The love that we talk about always has limits. There's always a tolerance limit. Sometimes the circumstance is so hard and bullshit that the so-called love for yourself collapses. And you fuck it all again and you try to kill everybody, including yourself. So, this love is fun but there's nothing in it.

Q: I wasn't talking about the relative love. When we look at Ramana, what do we see coming from his eyes?

K: After five hours of kitchen work, I'd look like him too. [Laughter] Why make him special?

Q: I'm not making him special...

K: Of course you make him a special old man with a special radiation of peace! But peace has no radiation. Silence never radiates. For who? There's nothing that comes out of Silence... to who?

Q: Come on Karl...

K: Come on! I tell you.

Q: If anyone would see that man, every one would recognize it...

K: That's the fucking problem, that everyone likes it.

Q: Aren't you here because of that as well?

K: I'm here to make an opposite. [Laughter] At least I try that everyone hates me. I try my best but I don't succeed. [Laughter] I try to offend everybody and still people look at me with wonder. [Laughter]

So, That what you are cannot be killed. And I totally love that you can do whatever when you are What you are because it doesn't make any difference. You are recognized by your intuition anyway. And there's no difference, you can be the biggest asshole and they still like you because you are What you are and not because you behave as a nice guy and you have lovely words [Mocking] I love you from my deepest core of my heart. Fuck it all! I hate it! I hate my core!

Q [Another visitor]: Can I ask something?

K: No! [Laughter]

Q: Okay, tell me when I should...

K: I'll tell you when you should... [Laughter]

Q: It reminds me of Shakespeare – How to tame a bitch...

K: The way to tame a bitch is put her on a beach and leave her alone. [Laughter]

Q: I just saw that our true nature is Love...

K: John Lennon said Love is just a four letter word. [Laughter]

Q: What?

K: Your earrings keep you away from hearing. [Laughter]

Q: In all the traditional pictures, Shiva and Vishnu all wear earrings... [Laughter]

K: [Laughing] You're bringing joy to this world.

Q: [Laughing] That's the story of this bitch...

K: When you're a bitch you have to decorate yourself, like a Christmas tree.

Q [Another visitor]: Intuition makes people like someone and not others?

K: I try to get rid of the people but they still come because here there's no one who tries to change them... so, they just can be as they are or not. No one gives a fuck of how they are and where they come from and what they're doing. This carelessness is more than enjoyable because that is what you are. No one gets a special treatment here. No one is trying to transmit some bullshit love or something. [Laughter]

Q: What is intuition?

K: That what you are by intuition is what it is in spite of transmitting anything. And you know it by heart that whoever wants to transmit something, wants to control you – you know that. And you are not here for control, you are here because you want to get rid of slavery because you are really fucked up by the experience of being a slave of something. Even being a slave of love is too much! That's why you enjoy this – fucking love, who needs it? This joy of... [exhaling deeply]... I don't have to enjoy myself to be myself. I don't have to love myself to be myself. This is *more* than enjoyable! This is like [exhaling deeply] stones dropping from your bloody heart that you don't even have.

I'm not here to put more stones and more heavy stuff on your so-called being. You're already loaded with all those ideas of how you have to be. Everyone says that first you have to love yourself before you can love everyone else on this Earth. All that bullshit. You know that you cannot love yourself because every morning when you wake up there's unconditional hate. [Laughter] Then for the whole day you try to love yourself and you are so exhausted at night that you fall asleep thinking, maybe tomorrow, but not today. You know that. That's why I say, you cannot love what is false. Loving is an artificial experience. You cannot trust it, it's always doubtful. You cannot love it. As much as you try to love it, you cannot... it's impossible! And because of that you seek a way out. You try to find what is true, what is real. But you always look in the wrong place because you're That what is real but not what you find.

So, *be* what you are what can never be lost or found in anything. And that doesn't need to be called anything. Just be that what you cannot *not* be and that is in spite of whatever you imagine or not – what you are. So, I destroy all of that, call it Love, call it Heart, call it whatever... I give a shit what you call it! Just be that what is That... and this peace you cannot disturb. You cannot *doubt* that... there's no doubt in it! This doubtlessness of your existence you cannot disturb and no one can disturb you as that. But everything else can be disturbed. All concepts of love and having an open heart... there will always be someone who wants to test you. How open is your heart really? How much can you take? How far does your acceptance go? What is your tolerance limit? The moment you say, 'I have an open heart, my tolerance is unlimited, I am infinite'... everyone is always around. Consciousness doesn't allow you to be one with your open heart for long. Maybe for a short while, but then it closes it for you, if you like it or not. [Laughter]

I mean it! It's not allowed. It cannot happen that there's one with an open heart. Ha ha, let's see what I can do! [Laughter] You get a new girl friend or you have to live with your mother and then you're sure that your heart gets closed again – just to defend yourself. [Laughter]

Q [Another visitor]: Because if you say there's an open heart, then there's also a closed heart...

K: Yes. How can there be an open one if there's no closed one? Both are concepts.

Q: So, what is real?

K: What you are. But you'll never *know* that. You have to be That what is real without knowing what is real and what is not real, because That what is real doesn't need to know what is real and not real. And that what needs to know what is real and what is not real, is unreal! That's the pointer!

So, be that what never needs to be real and has no idea about reality... maybe that's Reality, that which doesn't need to know what is reality and what is not. And that what needs to know what is reality for sure is artificial and false. What to do? What *not* to do? Try everything and fail. You will fail anyway, enjoy the failing. You realize yourself in failing. You will fail forever. You failed *not* to wake up! Now you woke up, awareness happened and the whole drama started. You now try to fix the problem which came by itself and will go by itself. It's not in your hands!

You are the Almighty, the Parabrahman, that what is Energy itself... and it cannot even control Itself... imagine! There's no two. In the nature of what you are, there's no second. Non-duality means where there's no second, there's no way of controlling yourself. Control needs two, love needs two, all of that needs two... but all of that is imaginary!

What you are cannot control Itself because there's no second that can control the absence of the first. What to do? Krishna says, 'I am the architect of the whole manifestation but the blueprint is already done and I cannot change what is already done. Now it's too late'. Everyone reads the Mahabharata but they look at the fighting but this single statement... the Absolute Almighty Krishna cannot change his own creation! Then who do *you* think you are? If even He cannot change that war has to happen, that you have to kill, that whatever is meant to happen will happen because it's already in the blueprint of whatever is there. So what? Who is this guy who thinks he can maybe change the world and has an idea of what is better and what is good and trying to do something.

Q [Another visitor]: So, too late means there's a time sequence?

K: Whatever happens already happened before it happens! That you cannot understand because the moment you understand, you disappear! You cannot allow that understanding to happen because in that understanding there's no 'me'. Understanding of 'me' can only happen when you think you can do something today or tomorrow. There's a doership, that you can change something. Without that idea of change you cannot remain as 'me', as a doer. Ownership can only remain when you believe that you have a free will and you can change your life. Without that there's no 'me'. If life is already lived, where can be the 'me' in it? There's just life living, which is already lived. There's silence. Even in living, there's silence because whatever happens next, already happened!

So, nothing comes in coming and nothing goes in going. But who can remain in that? No one. That kills you! If you call that Reality, then Reality kills you... just by being Reality! Just be That what you are and you kill the *idea* of what you are, *instantly*! In a split second, you split all ideas of a second. There's no one, there's not even *one*, because even one is one too many! By being What you are, there's not even one... and when there's no one, there's no second, because it needs one that there can be a second. But when you are That what is not even one, where can there be a second? Where can there be the love or lover or the beloved when there's not even one who could be the lover?

I try very hard to talk you into it. But it depends on you *being* it and not by my talking.

Q [Another visitor]: When the false sees the false as false...

K: When the false sees the false as false, does the false still see false as false? So, see the false as false as even the false sees false as false. [Laughter]

Q: Does fear disappear?

K: Nothing disappears. You're just what you are that cannot fear itself because there are no two. Does fear disappear? For who? For 'me'? And who cares if the fear disappears for the 'me'? Only me and the other me's. Only any 'me' is excited because it is in enemy land – any 'me', enemies, especially the first enemy. It can only survive in war, in worries, me, me, me. If I don't fear, I feel better.

No. It doesn't work... it's all too late. All what you can achieve now doesn't make you the chief. You're already Shiv, you don't have to become it. In India, they call it Shiv and not Shiva. You're already the Shiv but you want to achieve something, that's the stupid idea. You're the Shiv and you want to achieve yourself. What a joke! What a funny bullshit! You want to become the boss but you're *already* the boss! But the problem with the boss is that the boss has no soldiers. This is a military exercise but there are no soldiers. [Laughter] And no one listens to whatever you say, not even you. You give orders but no one follows them, not even you. You promise yourself all the time... tomorrow I'll be different! But what happens? Nothing. [Laughter] So many promises you give to yourself – orders – never again... I'll never fall into that trap again! I'll never get into any fucking relationship again, not me! [Laughter] And then around the corner someone comes and you say, 'Oh, that's destiny'. [Laughter] Then you say what can I do about Karma? One more time.

Q: If I realize myself as That what I cannot *not* be, is that a realization as well?

K: When 'you' realize, there's one too many who's realizing himself. If it really would be That which is realizing itself, there would be no 'one' who's realizing himself. But when you say, 'I' am realizing myself, it's already too late. It doesn't work.

Q: So, it can't be different...

K: What can't be different?

Q: If I can't change anything, it can't be any other way...

K: There's still one too many who cannot change anything. Forget it! You're too late now.

Q: But...

K: Whatever you say... but don't try to make me confirm whatever you say, because whatever needs a confirmation for sure is false. You should just say it without looking for a confirmation, don't ask me if it's right or wrong. Just say something without expecting a confirmation.

Q: I know I always look for confirmation...

K: I know and that comes from falsity. Only the false needs to be confirmed that what the false is saying is true. If I would care that someone confirms what I say and is pleased about it, I would not be in the right place.

Q: It's always an absolute problem, needing a confirmation...

K: I know. Nothing is firm enough, so you need a con-firm-ation all the time. So, there's a confirmation needed that I cannot *not* be it... even that doesn't work! Nothing works! Failing, failing, failing...

Q [Another visitor]: [Wobbling head] This means nothing in India...

K: It means I don't know. If you ask anyone the way, everyone knows the way and ten Indians pointing to ten different locations because they cannot say I don't know. It's not in their language.

Q: Then they send you to a wrong place...

K: But they don't care. [Laughter] It's like the Indian gurus who say you have to go there and there. They'll never tell you 'I don't know'. That's why yoga was invented and all the techniques because they think they have to say... 'I know, you do this and this'... otherwise no disciples! Indians are gurus and they need disciples and people who believe in them and have faith in them. But even the Western gurus are like that. Maybe there's not much difference between the Indian and the Western gurus. Guru, guru...

Q [Another visitor]: I read a book in which Nisargadatta said Consciousness is your God and you must always repeat Guru, Guru....

K: In which book?

Q: I don't know...

K: You read the book you don't know? [Laughter]

Q: He said repeat this mantra – Guru, guru...

K: Yes. If you can only repeat this continuously and you can make it an unpronounced Guru, guru, guru, guru. You don't allow any other thought in your mind and you'll be fine! But then you can also say, shit, shit, shit, shit. [Laughter] That would be the same too. If you just have one thought, that kills all the other thoughts... and after a while you have no story anymore. If you keep repeating this mantra – shit – in your brain, then after a while there's no other thought any more, only shit remains. Then shit becomes chit. Then you are chit and there's no one in shit.

So, just have one thought, it doesn't matter if you call it God, guru or shit. If there's only one thought, then it's fine... *if* you could do that! And not, pasta, spaghetti, baguette... [Laughter] It's really hard for the French mind because it's interrupted by food. [Laughter] But shit is the best because whatever you think is shit anyway.

Q: But you cannot see shit as sat-chit-ananda....

K: But that's shit again... because you *are* shit and then you as shit, see something as no shit. You try to make something out of shit, it's amazing! [Mocking] I see everything as gold, the ornaments don't interest me any more, only gold, because I'm a woman. [Laughter] Thank God nothing works, even *that* doesn't work.

Q: Every day I give chance to stories like this one...

K: Every day she's open to new ideas.

Q: But maybe there's a day where I get bored with all the ideas...

K: It's a good retirement plan. I look at you and I see it.

Q: It's kind of a mirror isn't it? [Laughter]

K: I like the story of UG travelling in a plane. There was an American sitting next to him making small talk... asking him what he was doing. UG said, 'I'm retired'. From what? 'From retirement!'... then the American kept quiet, Otherwise you cannot shut them up, Americans make all these networking connections, just in case they need them. They have such a defined, calculating, businessman inside.

Q: That's everyone...

K: Everyone has a different way. French want to dominate you. [Laughter]

No, you cannot retire from What-you-are. That's the way you retire from retirement... it will never stop! Your idea of enlightenment is like a retirement idea. That after realizing yourself, you'll be quiet forever. What a retirement idea! Then there may be some who claim that they retired now because they're enlightened. For me, nothing ever happened. Then you say, 'Oh, I want that retirement plan too because that sounds peaceful'.

No, it doesn't work... nothing ever works. No way out! You have to realize yourself again and it will be stupid again. Trying not to make it stupid is the stupidest thing. So be stupid, when you're stupid. When you're not, you're not. But even being *not* stupid, is really stupid.

Q: But something worked for him [Pointing at Ramana's picture]...

K: No, he was the same... he said, 'Nothing ever happened for that what I am'. He had this death experience and then he was That which is in spite of life and then nothing ever happened before, during or after that! Nothing ever happened after that or before that for That what he is. So, it didn't work for him as it doesn't work for you! You're already That for which nothing happened... and by words you'll not become it. Thank God, it didn't work for him. But you believe it worked for him and then you wait for the same experience to happen to you so that you could be what you are. But you may wait forever! Maybe that experience is not for you? Maybe you have to be in *spite* of that experience What you are! Who knows? Or it may come in thousands of thousands of thousands of lifetimes. But you're not interested in that because you want it now!

Q [Another visitor]: Do you believe in lifetimes?

K: Absolutely! I believe in everything.

Q: And nothing?

K: It's a belief system. Why should I not believe in it? I believe in everything! I believe that everything is possible. Whatever *can* happen, *will* happen, even Ken Wilber. [Laughter] You have the highest intellect mind and then you crash... shit happens!

So, thank God that I talk like this now... and it can stop at any moment. If it stops, it will stop and I still have to be What I am. If I would depend on sitting here and talking like this, I would be in quite a shitty state. Then I have to start to say, 'I love you'. [Laughter] So, if I ever start like that, think I lost something. [Laughter]

Q [Another visitor]: Today is a good day to start, it's Valentine's day... [Laughter]

K: The monsters wait around the next story.

Q [Another visitor]: I would like to ask about God's will and astrology...

K: Now I'm interested. Did you find the birth date of God? [Laughter]

Q: Can astrology make me believe that I have no free will?

K: No. Because you'll still make it 'your' will that you believe it... then you say, now I know! Then you become like Socrates... now I know that I don't know! Before I had free will, and now I don't have one. Now I lost my free will! What then? Astrology showed me that I have no free will. Then Astrology becomes your new God... a new Guru. Then you have a teacher called Astrology that taught you that you have no free will. But there's still one too many who has no free will! You think there's an advantage?

Q: Yes...

K: Yes, there's a relative advantage. Maybe by believing in that, having faith in it, your life becomes more peaceful because you don't take it so much personal any more. So there's an advantage, I agree... but for whom? For that one who needs an advantage! So it confirms one who needs an advantage! Even by understanding you try to have an advantage. But it permanently confirms that there's one who needs one. Amazing! So the biggest advantage is still a disadvantage because there's one who needs it. Fuck it! It's a relative 'me' who needs a relative advantage and it will never be big enough for what you are. Because you always look for a bigger one, for more knowledge, for deeper understanding, for the truth that's really true, the deepest truth... 'From the core of my truth'. People talk and they claim that they're talking from the core of their existence and *you* talk from somewhere else maybe. And if you're around them you'll sooner or later talk from the same place. Wow! Fuck! All these advantages are what? Devil's work, I tell you. It's Lucifer tempting you – false promises.

Jesus was in the desert for forty days and the devil tempted him that he can give him all the knowledge, all the kingdoms, he can be the ruler of the whole universe, whatever he wants he can get it, whatever advantages he dreams of can be given by the devil. And Jesus just said, you cannot give me anything. There's no advantage needed for What I Am.. the kingdom doesn't need any advantage. The kingdom of Heart is complete as it is and never needs any advantage at all. So, just by being what you are, the devil cannot tempt you. It always tries to make empty promises again. This astrology is tempting you now with understanding, with relative advantages... 'If I see everything as God's will then I'll have a more peaceful mind'. Yes, you will have a more peaceful mind... but who has a mind now? And who minds that? And who needs an advantage? Try to find that bastard!

Then when you find him, you'll see that it's not worth being that bastard who needs an advantage. You already found yourself as a bastard that needs an advantage and you already want to get out of it. How to get out of that? And I can just point to your naked existence that never needs any advantage at all. The Absolute advantage is being what you are that never needs any advantage... and by not knowing any advantage, not knowing any disadvantage. But the moment you know an advantage, you create a disadvantage in the same moment. This is a creative, artistic, 'me'.

How to get rid of that intelligent bastard – the intellect? It always tries to find another trap to trap you... and it's very creative, this intellect God, this logo. It's always logical and deep and you always step again. The 'advantage' trap is the biggest! Even saying I don't need an advantage any more is the next advantage trap... 'I'm now that one who doesn't need any advantage'... that's the next trap! Better be that what was always That – whatever – which doesn't even have an idea of advantage or disadvantage or anything.

When I talk to myself, I see that it's impossible to not step into the next trap... you cannot fail! Even *not* stepping into the next trap, is the next trap! You become so clever, so intelligent, wisdom itself, blah, blah, blah... even wisdom is a trap, heart is a trap, love is a trap. What is *not* a trap? And you cannot miss any trap! How can you miss it? How can you *not* realize yourself as the next trap? You'll always be trapped by yourself. What you are is trapping you and who cares about being trapped by what one is? By being trapped by what one is, you're not trapped by anyone else, you're just trapped by That what you are! You are addicted to that what you are. You are a total junkie for yourself. But who cares about being junkie for what one is? You are a total addict to that what is the biggest addiction which you cannot get rid of – being addicted to what you are. You have to be what you are, no way out of it! And the next trap is just the next trap, so what? Does it make you more or less, stepping into or not stepping into it? In the next advantage, there's no advantage and in the next disadvantage, there's no disadvantage – that's all. For what you are, there's no such thing! But still you have to experience yourself as that and that.

You have to be in *spite* of all that. You're the raper, you're the raping and you're that what is raped. Most of the time it feels like a rape and sometimes when you accept it, it feels like love... but both are the same in Nature. So, *be* the raper, the raping and the raped by being That what you are... and by trying to make it a love affair, you try to control the raping, that's all... by trying to love the rape. But it will always feel like a rape! You don't want to wake up. If you could, you'd stay in deep-deep sleep. No one wants to wake up but when you woke up, it's too late, that's all! It's an accident and it already feels like a rape that you have to exist! What to do?

Now you're fed up with that existence and you want to find a way out of it. You become a seeker who thinks... 'When I'm enlightened, I don't have to wake up any more because I'm always awake!' All the tricks in your mind start.

Q [Another visitor]: But there's no way *not* to wake up...

K: No. You experience yourself as you wake up but that who is experiencing itself as he woke up, doesn't wake up in it. But you have to experience yourself as one who woke up. God has to experience god, but the god who's experienced by God is not God. That what God is experiencing as god, is not God, but he cannot avoid it! He has to experience himself as a creative god and then he creates all of this! But the creative god is already an imagination... it's like a dream starting.

But That what *is* God doesn't know any God. But the moment God knows God, it's too late! Then trying to know God is too much. Then you try to know this God deeper and deeper. But to know that you exist is already false. But then you make it more false by really trying to know it inside out. Then you just know the inside out of falsity – that's all. What does that make you? A knower of falsity. So, what to do? So, even the deepest of the deepest of the deepest experience of the truth, is false!

What am I doing here? I have no idea!

Q: You're here to tear us apart...

K: I try to pull the rugs that are not even there. I'm pulling all the fake homes, the false homes away. I destroy only false homes. You still believe in an enlightenment which is a home run.

Q [Another visitor]: The good and the bad system is collapsing...

K: It cannot collapse. You fear that it will not collapse. And you're right, it will never collapse. So, what's collapsing?

Q: I'm thinking now...

K: You read it somewhere and now you're repeating it, and now you're in trouble because you don't know where it comes from. You think there's anyone here who's *not* speaking out of hearsay? And having read something, or listened to somebody... or repeating what is already said before or phrases from some books? You think you're alone in that? Even this guy [Pointing to himself] is repeating himself infinitely from whatever some gurus have said something before. You think I'm original? Keep dreaming. I'd never claim to be original, that would be too much anyway. There would be one too many who's original! Thank God I don't have to invent anything. Everything is already there. Why should I create something what is already there? I'm much too lazy for that. I just steal from everywhere, even from myself!

Q: But this controlling...

K: ...is very bad. Controlling is the devil's work.

Q: That's for sure...

K: Only the devil needs to control God. Are you now the devil or God? What are you now?

Q: I don't know...

K: That's the deepest devil. The devil who doesn't know and by trying not to know controlling that what is knowledge. You think by that you're getting out of being a devil? Try harder! The fire will burn and where there's a devil there's fire, you know that. But that what you are is the coolest fire. There's not even a fire for What you are.

Come on... some more from the devil! I like to talk to the devil. It's always fun with the devil. [Laughter] The devil always thinks something needs to change. The devil only lives in changes. When there's silence... there's no God, no devil, no such things. So the Devil creates religion and all the imaginary Gods to be the master of this world. Amazing! All the religions come out of hell. Hellelujah! Where else should they come from? From that Absolute Silence nothing comes and nothing goes... only in hell there are changes.

So, relative life, the little god, the fallen angel, needs movement. It needs something to change. That's called mind, that's called 'me'! That's the devil's advocate... it cannot survive in silence so it makes sure that something has to happen. Something has to collapse, something has to break down, the falsity has to go, the ignorance has to be unveiled. Something has to happen, at least enlightenment! When and if this will happen and if I look through all that falsity, specially 'me', then I'll still be the devil. The devil is the phantom... it's already an imaginary, what? God knowing himself he becomes his own devil. And now he loves himself and now he wants to make his nature true, real. Whatever he tries now is futile! The devil always creates a hell... because without a hell, the devil cannot survive. What would the devil do without hell? And Hell means separation, hell means movement, hell means all the fake experiences, whatever you can experience. It's all fake coming out of a fake idea of 'I'. Fake, fake, fake! And you can fake it for a long time, I tell you, because you're surrounded by fake. The next fake needs your confirmation and you need the confirmation of the next fake. Fake, fake, fake, fake, fake!

The false always needs to be confirmed by false... so, better be that what never needs any confirmation at all.

Q [Another visitor]: But it's you who's saying that the false is the false. Whatever you are saying, we can turn the whole thing upside down and change the Absolute. There's no such thing that doesn't change. That's Buddhism, there's no such thing that doesn't change...

K: But first be That what you are and then we talk again.

Q: But it changes...

K: No. That what you are doesn't change. Don't try it from a clever mind. I tell this to you again... it's very clever and very smart and very scholared. When you listen, I would never claim what I say is the truth. I always say it's bullshit. But now you claim that what you say is truth.

Q: I'm just saying that whatever you say, the opposite to that can be true. I say that Absolute is what-is but what-is is change. We can never know what it is from this side anyway. So, what difference does it make if we say whatever it is. Since we are not That and there's no way in and no way out, why shouldn't what I say about the Absolute be true?

K: If you like... you think I would care about your confirmation?

Q: At least it allows me to be where I am...

K: Then just be it... but don't bother me! [Laughter] I mean it... if you're so confirmed and established in that what you just said, then be it and just leave me alone. I tell you, if you really would be established in your perfect understanding, just go home and watch television... but don't bother me! I'm not here to fight any windmills or nice turning wheels of understanding. I destroy everything, even what I say, you know that. It's not that I try to find a perfect system.

Q: No, there's no perfect system...

K: But you just wanted to create one right now.

Q: Yeah...

K: Yeah, yeah, yeah... [Laughter] and gathering all the big stuff around, Buddhism and all the help from all sides just trying to make your point. How much help do you need to make that point? I'm just innocently asking. [Laughter]

Q: And I'm just innocently saying... [Laughter]

Q [Another visitor]: Yesterday you called us advanced seekers...

K: Never! [Laughter] I just said this arrogance of the advanced seekers walking around the mountain. I didn't call *you* an advanced seeker, for sure not! All the so-called advanced seekers come here because they think they're looking for truth and not for football.

Q: Yesterday you mentioned that the primal fear we had was not dying when we die. That never occurred to me. I'm just wondering what would the second fear be, so that I maybe relate to that one... [Laughter]

K: You want more... you fear that the satisfaction never comes. That you look for peace and peace will never happen. So, satisfaction may never come. Even that is part of the primal fear that in death you don't die... because you imagine that death brings you peace. So, you fear that death doesn't bring you peace. The basic fear is that even death cannot bring you what you're looking for. So, you fear that this longing for peace will not stop... and I confirm you. You have to be in spite of that What you are and not because something brings you peace, come on! But your idea that death will bring you the final peace is a mirage. And you fear that and you know it by your intuition that it will not be there. You know it but you just turn away from it because you fear that what you already know. It's amazing!

Q: Or stupid?

K: It's not stupid, it's just that you cannot accept it... and no one ever accepted that!

Q: Is that part of the defence system?

K: No, that's why I make this meditation on the absence, because when you experience already that the absence cannot bring you that what you're looking for, then you don't wait for it. Even the absence cannot bring you the peace that you're looking for. Normally absence will be less – the absence of life, the absence of living, the absence of movement. Then even when the absence cannot give you the peace you're looking for, then there's no peace in the absence – neither in the presence or absence! Then you just rest what never needs to rest anyway, because now you have the idea that you have to rest in something, you have to find your final home. That makes you restless. But if you look for it and you go into that absence of movement and life, that what you call death, then even death cannot bring you what you're looking for. Then you rest in that What-you-are... and that What-you-are never needs to rest in anything and that what needs to rest, was always false!

But you have to look at this yourself that even the absence

cannot bring you the peace! That even in death, you cannot rest in peace. So, even the peace cannot bring you the peace. You say absence is peace I agree... but even peace cannot bring you the peace you're looking for and that you fear most! You're right, you *should* fear because peace cannot be bought by anyone. The peace you experience, is not the Peace you are. So, peace-off. [Laughter]

Q: Now I'm depressed...

K: I hope! This is a total void of hope, but What-you-are has no problem with it... but what you're not, disappears in it! You cannot bear that void of hope. You need hope. You *need* the hope that when I die at least then I can rest. There are so many tombstones, 'rest in peace'. But you cannot rest in peace, what you are cannot rest in peace. It never *needs* to rest in peace because What-you-are *is* Peace... and never needs to rest in anything. This bloody hope! All these religions are made by hope and hope comes from the devil. It needs time, it needs future, it needs whatever this devil needs to get your attention. So, there's no peace for you – Hallelujah! Enjoy it, there'll never be any peace for anyone and the peace you can get is a piece of cake. But the piece of cake cannot satisfy you. Thank God! Enjoy that nothing can satisfy you, not even peace. The highest, even that what is the nothing, the Absence, the Holy Spirit, whatever you call it... even the peace of the Holy Spirit is empty!

You're here to be killed! Or are you here for having a nice time... imagining that peace comes anyway when I die? I'm here for retirement. You have to retire from the idea that you can ever retire. That's why I make all these jokes so maybe you can bear it a little bit. So that you don't collapse. But you'll never collapse because you're the Energy itself. How can you collapse? You're inexhaustible in your nature! How can you exhaust yourself, even in peace? Even peace cannot exhaust you.

Q: So, I cannot walk around the mountain?

K: No. Why do you want me to confirm that you breathe? What an idea. Is it still okay that I breathe? [Laughter] No, it's not okay that you breathe.

Q: You know, I can put up a sign that I'm not advanced and walk around...

K: That's very advanced... it's like saying I'm not arrogant. But this message is quite... whatever. Look at it! How many times did you experience this peace in absence? And did it last? You're still restless. Every experience is a restless experience. Then there's sometimes a temporary pause that you call peace. And then? Comes again. The dream continues. As long as you have a head, it's unbearable.

Q: But if there's real peace...

K: There's no real peace. Fuck your real peace! You again make it a bloody hope for a moment of time. Peace doesn't know any peace. There's no need of real peace for Peace!

Q: We're just talking about peace...

K: No. We are not 'just' talking about peace, you wanted to make it a special thing again. I know you, I know everybody. [Laughter] The devil always makes an attempt again... 'If there's real peace...'

Q: Then you wouldn't remember...

K: There's no 'then'. Who is now that remembers? And who is then who does not? Show me one who's here now, then you show me the one who's there not. Then... postponing again for an imaginary whatever! And calling it 'real' peace... maybe a green peace! [Laughter] This tricky thing never stops. It tries to create another one and another one, and the truth of the truth, truthy, truthy, truthy, truthy. This fake Brahma always tries to say that there must be an end of the light of Shiva... I found it! Then he shows off that I found the end of the light and the beginning of the light of Shiva because I'm Awareness and I'm the beginning and the end. I found the beginning and I found the end of that light of Shiva – 'me'! Then I talk to you from the deepest truth of my innermost being. Yuck! [Grunting] Then I really get angry and destroy... like Jesus going to the temple and getting all the temple tax collectors... especially when I hear the deepest core of my heart. I love you all!

[groaning] [Laughter]

It's amazing when you see that even *that* comes from the devil's underground... wonderful! How creative this bastard is. I adore him actually for that. And he tries again and again and he cannot make anything. He has no power. He tries again and again and creates another trap so that you step in but he cannot do anything. He works his arse off for nothing! [Laughing] Bloody intellect! And you cannot get rid of the intellect because you are intellect, when there's intellect. *Intellect* – ah, what a *lecture*!

So, what to do? Enjoy the devil. You can only enjoy the devil in hell because What-you-are, you cannot enjoy. So what? And What-you-are doesn't need to be enjoyed by you, so enjoy whatever you can enjoy! That what you can enjoy cannot bring the joy of What-you-are. Final! Know whatever you can know – the knower, the knowing and whatever-can-be-known. But no knower and no knowing and nothing that can be known can deliver the Knowledge you are. It cannot make you That!

So, enjoy that... whatever! Enjoy the heart you don't have. I mean it! Enjoy the love you don't need. Enjoy! Enjoy yourself, because it will take a while. Longer than you can imagine. If *you* don't enjoy yourself, there's no *other* self... brm, brm, brm...

Q [Another visitor]: The sixty-three saints that walk around the mountain...

K: They don't walk around the mountain. [Laughter] Now you want to know where do I meet them and on which time? [Laughter]

Q: Is Jesus there?

K: No. It's only the ones with underwear. [Laughter] What do you expect from them?

Q: You mentioned Sai Baba is one of them so I was wondering who are the other sixty-two?

K: There are books... read them! Why do you ask me? I'm not an oracle here. Lazy bastards! They think Karl is here so why should

I read anything? [Laughter] Why should I invest myself? I sit here anyway and Karl may know. Ha ha ha! Women ask you anything... especially how are you today? Then you have to find how you are. [Laughter] Don't say anything wrong because she cooks for you, you have to find the right answer... Yeah, okay! [Laughter] Tricky questions all the time. You meet a friend and you ask him, 'How are you', just to check if he's on top or under you. If he's in a good shape, you say – yeah, yeah okay. If he's not in a good shape you get excited – Oh! You're not so good today. [Laughter] It's like in a war, you check out your enemy before you shoot.

Q [Another visitor]: I have a personal and a practical question...

K: I don't answer personal or practical questions. I know those questions, they always want to put you in a straight jacket.

Q: It's not a personal question about you, it's a personal question about me...

K: It's the same.

Q: Not even practical?

K: No. I'm not here for therapy questions. Practical is therapy.

Q: Should I stay or should I go?

K: You should jump out of the window if you ask me... at least then I don't have to see you anymore. [Laughter] It's always amazing, the moment you ask them to jump... No! Not me! [Laughter] If someone says that he is jumping and you try to stop him, he still insists on jumping.

I must have said this story a thousand times. My father wanted to kill himself when my mother died. He was crying after the funeral, 'My beloved wife is gone, I want to kill myself'. I asked him, 'What can I do for you? Gun? Rope?' He could not believe it. He looked at me and he was really furious, his son wanting to help him in that way. I was ready to help him, 'Should I go to your cousin next door because he's a hunter. Can I get you a gun or something?' He became so angry that he forgot to kill himself!

[Laughter] Then in the same evening he was drinking with his friends. Then three months later there was another widow whose husband died a month earlier. They had a party and were drunk on the way home... since then they are a couple. But three months earlier, he wanted to kill himself and he meant it. You cannot trust anyone! Now we're talking about love. He was the first man for my mother and she was the first woman for him and nothing went wrong during the marriage. Whenever I came back from the party, he always caught me and yelled, 'You son of a whore'. Later I knew where I got it from! [Laughter]

Don't trust anyone! No one can help himself! There will be some circumstance that dictates and the biggest love collapses in one second! There's a song from Johnny Cash, 'And then there is darkness...' Out of the blue, things turn into darkness. The most delightful love and trust and faith in the relationship. Then there is one moment and it drops into darkness by whatever... and you cannot avoid it. Fuck! What an unpredictable life! But I like it that way. You can never know what will happen next. You cannot trust this guy who is the very self in any moment – neither inside nor outside. There's no way to trust yourself, not even your guru because even *he* cannot help himself!

And I like it most... these stories from Muktananda and Ramesh Balsekar. I like that no one can control life. No one is saint enough. Life will always make sure that it breaks you down. And you can write so many letters to God. [Laughter]

Q [Another visitor]: Shaktipat also comes from the devil who wants to control?

K: Yes – everything! Devil means God knowing himself as consciousness... and consciousness is trying to control consciousness. That's called God trying to control God... God trying to know God, but only because it thinks that by knowing himself he'll get peace. God wants to make peace with himself but the more he wants to make peace with himself, he fights for it! It's always counter- productive. The war will never stop! Whatever you can experience is an experience of hell because hell means separation. You cannot experience yourself without that. Any experience, as deep or as high it may be, whatever you can say, is hell because hell means two. It needs an experiencer and something to experience. Even the absence experience is an absence of an experience of an experiencer, which it is not What-you-are.

You experience yourself as an experiencer but you're not that what you experience. The experience of an experiencer is what you can call God - the God experience. But the God experience is not that what is God... so, what to do? You can only realize yourself as hell, in separation, because you can only experience yourself as a seer that is different from that what is seen... an experiencer different from what he's experiencing, there is no other way! Even the experience of absence needs one who's different from absence. So, the peace you can experience can only be a relative experience, as deep as it can be, as profound as it can be. The understanding you can have needs one who understands. It needs an experience of understanding. But the experience of understanding, cannot be That.

So, I don't mind hell because that's the way you realize yourself... you cannot otherwise. How otherwise can Parabrahman dream himself? He can only dream himself as a dreamer dreaming, a knower knowing. But already the knower is part of the dream. The creative God is already part of the creation. And whatever comes out of it, is part of it! So, the dream cannot unmake you, and it cannot make you, so just be That... and not by any understanding you will become it. I can only repeat, by whatever... you cannot *attain* What-you-are... in that way, you're unattainable! All attaining is in the dream. And all whatever is are empty promises... and you have to follow them.

It's always pro-missing... and I sit here and say enjoy the missing, enjoy that you miss yourself in all those experiences. Don't suffer about the best that is there because in that you're not there. You have to enjoy yourself as that what is always missed in anything, because What-you-are is never in any circumstance. In whatever deep experience, you are not there!

Q [Another visitor]: So, you're saying, any experience is not it!

K: I don't say it's not it. It's a realization of What-you-are but you cannot find yourself in your realization – that's all. I don't say it's not... I just say Reality and realization are not different but Reality cannot be found in realization because it was never lost in it! The Nature of realization is Reality. But now you try to find a 'special' reality and that makes it a problem. You want to make it 'your' reality, your special reality. Then it becomes ownership shit. Out of that Reality comes a shit reality.

Q: But the seeking never stops anyway?

K: It never started! There *was* no seeking. There's no Reality in a seeker, there's no Reality in seeking, there's no Reality in what can be sought. So, there's no such thing as seeking – especially no 'seeker'.

Q: And this mirage is going to continue?

K: There's no mirage in that sense... there's only Reality realizing itself, Life living. If you call it a mirage then there would be something that's *not* a mirage. You always create differences. There's just life living. There's just Reality realizing itself; and you have to realize itself – finished! So, be That what you cannot *not* be and that has to realize itself. What else can I point to?

Q: Are you pointing to something that has no landing place?

K: Even that is too much landing... then you land in not landing! The worst place that you can land in, is that place where you cannot land in. All what you can say, is intellect. What would be the advantage in not landing? For who? Question again. Does Reality need *not* to land to be Reality? Reality can land infinite times, and in landing not landing, and in departing not departing. It cannot go away from What-it-is... there's no danger in anything.

Land when you land or don't land when you don't land. So what? All is empty. Otherwise you make it like not landing is better than landing. What's the problem with landing?

Q: I'm trying to maintain the continuity of emptiness...

K. Even that is not a problem, try! Do you think it makes you more or less? Try it! You have so much time. [Laughter] If nothing can give you rest anyway, you can do whatever... or not. If nothing is done by doing and nothing is done by not doing, what's the problem? But no one can be it for you. If there's one problem at all, it is that no one can be it for you... not even 'you'. Because you always try to find 'one' who can be it for you. Then you follow his footsteps. Then you make it a biography of one... whatever... because you need a biography. Astrology, which stars? Jupiter has to be in the eighth house otherwise I cannot become what I am. [Laughter]

Some say that, if you don't have your Saturn in that constellation, you can never make it. You have to wait until the next time and then you have to be born in the right moment. You have to resist to come out before that moment is. [Laughter] But sometime it's really too long. Or you have to find the right guru. There's no such thing as a right guru, every guru you find is false, Thank God! Especially gurus you can find! [Laughter] Then they say that the guru has to find *you*. [Yawning] [Laughter] Then you're the chosen one... 'Look the guru found me!' You devote yourself, you give your one and only vote to the mountain, 'I found a guru who gives a shit about my existence'. I like that. That's why I like the mountain because it doesn't care if you're the devotee of the mountain or not. That's why maybe the mountain is a good guru because it gives a shit about your existence! You can walk around a thousand times, or never, you think the mountain cares? Otherwise you have a kilometer counter... if I make two hundred thousand meters then I get a gold medal, Arunachala gives me a special gift. [Laughter]

No! Carelessness – come on! The one and only guru is carelessness of existence itself. Arunachala is just a symbol for that. It's not the mountain, it's the carelessness of the mountain who is the guru.

Q [Another visitor]: What is the enjoyment about the fact that there's no end to this?

K: Then I don't have to look for it. I enjoy to be lazy, that's all. Because laziness is joy. But looking for an end is hard work. Then you cannot find it and you're really disappointed and frustrated that you cannot find the end... total frustration in not finding the end – I worked my arse off and I couldn't find the end. Then I turn around and try to find the beginning and fuck it! I couldn't even find the beginning [Laughter] Whoah!

So, just be lazy... you're anyway the lazy bastard, so why not *be* one? God is a lazy bastard, he's too lazy to know himself. That's the nature of laziness. He's even too lazy to know himself... then there's a joy of not needing to know yourself. But now you know yourself and you work your arse off to *not* know yourself. But it doesn't work. It's too late. Now you know yourself and you still have to be That what never needs to know himself by knowing yourself. [Groaning]

Thank you for going. [Laughter]

14th Feb 2016
Tiruvannamalai

CHAPTER FOUR

What You Gain, You Lose Again

Q: What is Grace?

K: A fucking idea! If you ask the question, what is Grace, it's already too late.

Q: Why do we talk about it?

K: You just have to talk about something. Forget grace and be that what you are and that is grace.

Q: It's tricky...

K: It's not tricky, it's very easy. Forget grace and be that what you are and that is grace. And by forgetting what you are and what you are not, you are That what *is* grace. But that grace doesn't know any grace and doesn't show any grace and never needs any grace. So, it's not for 'you'.

Q: But we're all waiting for grace to come...

K: That's the joke! Grace is waiting for grace to happen but grace will never happen! So what? You'll wait forever for Grace to happen. Waiting for Godot, it's like waiting for God. But God will never show up. So what to do? God or Buddha never shows himself, never walked this earth. It will never come as an experience. You wait for something what will never happen because That what is grace is not part of any happening.

Q: I think people shouldn't just talk about it...

K: Why not? Then you make it special again. But it's never special, it's the most ordinary what-you-are... it's never special. If you *not* talk about it, you make it even more special.

Q: But what is it?

K: It's not an object that we can talk about. So be that what is not even a subject: there's neither subject nor object. What would you get out of it if you knew what it is? Would you then control it or put it in your pocket and show it to someone? Thank God it cannot be owned by anyone... you can only *be* it but you can never *have* it. Drop the mind and then you're fine!

Q: But it's only by grace that we can drop the mind...

K: It's not by grace, it's by being what you are and that is Grace. *Being* grace and not *having* any grace and not *needing* any grace... and by that you drop the 'my' grace.

Q: I thought you were going say migraine...

K: Yeah. You may get a migraine when you're still looking for grace. Then you're graining and graining. You want to make cheese out of the milk and think that cheese is better than milk. The Buddhists say that you need to churn so much that you make butter out of milk of existence. You need to make a lot of effort, the entire Milky Way becomes butter or cheese. From that place you can just jump out of existence. [Laughter] It's like a frog in a jar filled with milk. Then they say that the frog has to make a lot of movements for milk to turn into butter. From the butter it becomes the Buddha. [Laughter] A Buddha that jumps out of its own... what?

It's all Vedanta or a Buddhist idea that you have to *do* something. That you can do it, that there's a way out of it.

Q: Is there something out there that will come and do it for me? [Laughter]

K: You're in a mixer already and you wait for the energy to switch on? Then you wait for grace that someone can turn the switch on. If you wait for Grace to come you'll wait forever I tell you.

Q: You bring me back to hopelessness now...

K: You belong there. [Laughter] I don't have to bring you back there. She wishes to be dead but her primal fear is that she doesn't die when she dies. That's why she's sitting here, otherwise she would've already killed herself. I think that's true for many of the seekers. If you really would be sure that it would be the end, maybe you'd just do it. But you're not. Then you fear that maybe the next one is worse than this one. That's why you see what can you do in *this* life.

Q: I wouldn't want to go through all those teenage days again...

K: You think you ever came out of it? [Laughter] Look at you, don't you ever look in the mirror? [Laughter]

Every relationship is really doubtful. No one knows if he really wants it or not. It's always like – What am I doing here? What's going on? Especially relationship with yourself – Should I have one? Shouldn't I have one? Do I really love myself or hate myself? What's going on today? Today I try to hate myself, maybe it works better than loving myself. It's too late because it's re-late... 'you' re-late to someone and it's already too late.

Q [Another visitor]: What is the nature of doubt?

K: You! [Laughter] I mean it, the phantom 'you', that you exist, that you are – that's doubtful. That's the nature of doubt.

Q: And out of these doubts...

K: The doubt is producing a doubt, that's all. You know that this is not real and then you doubt, both come together. Then you try to get out of that doubtful existence. Then whatever you do you confirm that there's someone in doubt. There's no way out of it.

How can that what has to exist, which is the root of doubting, get out of that doubt? How can the unreal become real?

Q: Can it die?

K: How can it die? It's not real. How can that what is not there die? Come on! Get real. How can something die what is not even there? How can an imagination disappear? Tell me.

Q: In deep sleep there's no...

K: Now you imagine a deep sleep already. Trying to find a way out of presence of a doubtful 'I' and imagining that in deep sleep I'm not. So I now better imagine to be in deep sleep? Or is it not too late when you imagine deep sleep? Then even deep sleep becomes a concept.

Q: There's some intuition that...

K: Who has an intuition? Even the intuition is doubtful because it comes from a doubtful one who has an intuition.

Q: Not now...

K: Who is speaking now?

Q: Self...

K: You think?

Q: Yes...

K: You think you think? [Laughing] Sounds good. There's one who thinks that he thinks. Wonderful! And you think that out of thinking comes another thinking? You're swimming in a septic tank and you want to get out of it.

Q: Burning the doubt...

K: You want to swallow it and make the tank empty. Then you think that by drinking the water you make the septic tank empty and then you are purified? But then the water is all in you. All the shit is in you. You're surrounded by purity but all the shit is in you. [Laughter] That's like karma yoga, you want to clean all the world but by you cleaning it you are sucking it all in yourself. Then the shit is somewhere else but you don't see it anymore because what's inside you, you don't see and what you imagine what you don't see, doesn't exist. Ha ha ha!

So what is this idea of purification? It is one of the dirtiest ideas you can have. It makes you dirty inside but you look very nice outside, very pure, very white, walking around like pure innocence. There's no spot on the outside - but don't look inside. But we have many of these so-called good people shining from outside, all in white, innocently dressed, always smiling, no bad feelings, 'I love you all'. [Laughter] I cannot harm any fly. What is all about that? In America and India many of the gurus are sitting in the prison because they committed so many crimes - but on the outside they preach purity and doing something what's right. Then you find them in the newspaper being imprisoned again. In Christianity, in monasteries and schools, sooner or later you find out paedophile cases everywhere, but from the outside they're really Holy Spirit. So what about doubtful actions and appearances? It appears to be, whatever... but it's just an appearance.

So, what is doubtful? Whatever you can talk about is doubtful.

Q: What about feelings?

K: Feelings are the same, they're just thoughts. Who calls energy as feelings? Only the mind. Without mind there's no emotion. It needs one who defines an emotion and has emotions and knows what it means. It's a hearsay... like this feeling is called 'anger'. I didn't know it before but now I know that it's not so good, because people tell me it's not so good. So what should I do with it? I have to repress it. I have to work on my anger. It's *all* a hearsay! So, what to do?

[Starts eating a banana]

Only the banana is white from inside. [Laughter] And the wife of Eckhart Tolle, she's white from inside as well. She told me that her grandma called her 'Banana' because she's Chinese from outside and white from inside, just like a banana. That makes Eckhart a

Tarzan. [Laughter]

[Pointing to a visitor]

I saw a big flyer of your friend, seems like he made it. [Laughter]

Q: The bigger the flyer, the bigger the guru...

K: Yeah. That's called a bigger 'me'. I'm always surprised people think truth needs advertisement. I always thought only shit needs advertisement, like McDonalds and Coca Cola. But shit is the biggest master anyway because so many flies cannot be wrong. No guru ever had more disciples than shit. [Laughter] And it's nourishing, ask the flies. They jump like seekers on *samadhis*. Everyone wants to drink honey, I say just be shit. [Laughter]

Q [Another visitor]: Can you talk about *vasanas*?

K: I started the talk by talking about the septic tank. You work out your *vasanas* outside but you just put them into a bag somewhere.

Q: What about transformation?

K: Transformation only means that you put them from one place to another place.

Q: It means turning it from one state to another...

K: You think that you can make gold out of shit. That's an alchemist's idea that you can make gold out of shit, but not by purifying it. You have to see the gold in shit by just seeing the nature of shit which is gold. That's getting rid of all the vasanas at once. That's the direct way of getting rid of all the shit, by just seeing the essence of it. Otherwise you work your arse off for nothing. You just shift from one to another one.

Q: And there's no end?

K: There's no end to it. Karma yoga is like unknotting one knot and making place for ten others. Just be the shit because that what you are *is* shit. But That what is shit doesn't know any shit. So, by knowing yourself you are that what is shit but that what is shit doesn't *mind* any shit. But don't be someone who *sees* shit because that makes you a special shit. Then you think you're not shit and that's really shitty.

So, who is really shit? It's that one who sees shit. Shit doesn't know shit and by not knowing shit, shit is knowledge. Then shit is chit. You transform shit into chit instantly by being That what you are. Otherwise you work and work and work. It's like Sisyphus rolling the stone up to the mountain which always rolls down again. When you're up at the mountain you want to enjoy it, 'I made it'. Then you let go of the stone and what does a stone naturally do? It goes back where it belongs – down. You want to take this body to the highest truth but you cannot. You have to leave everything behind otherwise you try to purify something that will never be pure enough.

Q [Another visitor]: There's a story about the dark side or the shadow...

K: There's an old Indian story about a guy who wants to get rid of his shadow. He digs a grave and goes deeper and deeper. At the deepest point there's no light and then he think there's no shadow and he made it. Then he closes it quickly and closes his eyes and is happy that he got rid of his shadow. But the moment he opens his eyes in daylight, what does he see? His own shadow over the grave. You cannot bury your shadow. You cannot get rid of your shadow because you are the light that creates shadows. What can you do? Even the experience of light is a shadow of yourself. That you have to see that even the light of Shiva is not Shiva. The Light doesn't know any light and the light that can be known is not Shiva. And the light that you can know creates darkness as well. When you experience light, you create darkness. But that what is light is not experienced by that. But if you believe by experiencing light that this is light and it is opposite of darkness, then that's relative light being opposite to darkness, or knowledge being opposite to ignorance.

Know yourself as that what *is* Light but there's no *experience* of light. No one can remain in That what one is because you can only be a 'me' in light when you have an idea about yourself. Now you want to be enlightened but whatever you do to try to be enlightened puts you more into darkness. So, what to do? You want to bring light into the darkness which is already there... because the Nature of darkness is Light and Nature of light is Light. But trying to bring light into darkness doesn't work.

Q [Another visitor]: The light that's mentioned here is the physical light. But what about the light of Consciousness?

K: Even that is relative light because you can name it – you can frame it. You can give it a name, like awareness. It's an experience, the purest notion of existence – Om – light and sound, the purest you can have. But even the purest is not pure enough for what you are. You are Purity itself and in that there's no idea of purity. And in that nothing is closer to you or nothing is apart from you. If the light of consciousness, like awareness, is closer to something what you believe in, then something else is further away. What kind of light is that which makes differences?

Consciousness always creates differences. The superior consciousness is light, the auro-bingo light, when all being is gone and only light remains. The sun and the experience of sun. But even the experience of sun is not the sun. Then they create a dark sun. The Nature of sun is like That what you are in the absence or in the presence. The absence would be darkness and the presence would be light. What you are experiences itself in darkness and in light, in consciousness and in unconsciousness, in presence and absence.

Q: Does God want to know itself?

K: As relative God, yes. As Absolute, no. So, yes and no. When God knows himself, he wants to know himself because God knowing God is a doubtful God. Then he wants to know God, his truth. So, the moment God knows God, he's looking for himself – out of love. That's the loving caring God, loving caring about itself, he cannot change that. That's like consciousness. Consciousness is like God knowing He's conscious and then it tries to know what is conscious – inquiring into that what it is – infinitely. That's why it's said that consciousness is a *realization* of what you are, but that what is your Reality, you cannot find in it. Whatever you make it closer, whatever it is, is a dreamlike... 'whatever'.

Q: No self!

K: That's called selfish because you fish for yourself in a septic tank. You become a fisherman fishing for yourself. The Self becomes a fish and you want to catch yourself. But you have to go to that self-is... Self *is*, not selfish! So, what to do? I try my best but it's not good enough. [Laughter] I'm happy that I'm never good enough. Actually I enjoy that I'll never be good enough because if I'd be good enough, that would be the end of everything. It doesn't work. So, it's not meant to be good enough because the moment it would be good enough, everything would be gone.

Q [Another visitor]: And?

K: You long for it but it would not happen. Jesus or Ramana, if those guys would have been good enough, everything would have ended instantly. If the Self would've ever found itself or would've realized its nature, there would be no continuation of this dream. So, it's impossible. What to do? Even the biggest guys, the biggest gurus, the biggest realized ones, didn't have any consequence. There's no consequence in anything. [Pointing to a visitor] But she's longing for it. She would not mind the whole universe to die now with her. Look at her! The rooster who wants to find the one and only corn which makes her disappear.

Everyone is like an addict, meditating, like taking drugs to kill himself and thinking if I do that and that, the world will stop and there will be no 'me' and no world... because everyone is fed up to exist. God is fed up. God wants to go home but he's always looking for a home somewhere where he cannot find it. God sitting here looking for a home. This is a home for the homeless here. What to do?

Q [Another visitor]: Can you tell me about the myth of the black sun?

K: It's being the absence of the presence of something, that's the black sun. The presence would be the experience of the light and the absence would be the experience of darkness, that's the black sun. The white light and the black light, it's like a spectrum. You experience yourself as a black sun and a white sun. So, you're the black sun and the white sun. When there's presence as light, you're the light. When there's absence as darkness, you're the darkness. But you're neither. Very easy.

Q: No...

K: You don't have to know what is the black sun, just be the black sun. You're not a son of anybody, you're the black son which has no mother. Now you believe yourself to be the black sheep, but you're just a black son. Otherwise you make a concept again that black sun is like that. It's the swastika in the reverse direction, it's light turning away from you and when the light turns away from you, you see the darkness, because you can only see light when the light particles come towards you. If it goes away from you, it's darkness. It's the same light but only the Seer is real. Only the Parabrahman, the Absolute Dreamer, the Seer himself is real. The rest is just different experiences. The two main experiences are the white sun and the black sun. The experience of light which is like a dream coming forward and the experience of darkness of the dream going away. But it's the same in essence.

Q [Another visitor]: But the experiencer is real...

K: Even the experiencer is not real. Only That what is experiencing the experiencer you can say is real. The experiencer is as unreal as what he's experiencing.

Q: But the experiencing is real?

K: No, even that is not real. If experiencing would be real than non-experiencing would be not real. Whatever you say is real, you create an opposite, you know that.

Q: Now you're going into the words. I'm talking about the

experiencing and not the words...

K: But for who? Who calls something experiencing?

Q: Again you're going into the words...

K: No, I'm not going into the words. You say something and I say whatever you're saying is not true, it's not the reality. That I say. Experiencing the 'I Amness' can be an experience.

Q: Drinking water...

K: Yes, that can be experienced. There's a drinker drinking water. So what? What's real in it? If that would be real, there should be permanently drinking water.

Q: Of course, only the seer is real...

K: No. The Absolute Seer is real, not the seer you can see and not the seeing and not what can be seen... because the seer seeing what can be seen is a scenery and the scenery is not real. But you want to make it special. As if knowing is good and it has to be without a knower and what can be known. Then you make knowing better than a relative experience of a knower knowing something what can be known. What do you want to do?

Q: I'm done... [Laughter]

K: People come to me because they're stuck in these ideas. They read it so many times with teachers, all this esoteric blah, blah, blah and now they think knowing is good and it's real. Then you land in something but then you have to depart again. What was before you said that knowing is real? Something else was real for you, so your reality is permanently changing. Then you give knowing another name for something. Permanently changing, this bastard. [Laughing] Always showing itself in a different form or an idea or a concept. Always covering itself with concepts otherwise it cannot survive. And the very nice ones are knowing and being – just *be* because being is good and being someone is bad. So, there's always bad and good. If you're *someone* who is being, than it's not good, if you're just *being* it's good. But for who? Tell me for who? Who needs that advantage that being is a better wellness existence and being someone is a nightmare?

The question is who needs to change the nightmare? What is living the nightmare and what is living a nice dream? There's nightmare when there's one in the dream and good dream is when there's no one in the dream and there's just dreaming? Dreaming is better than one dreamer who's dreaming? Who needs these landing places or definitions of something? That's the point! Who defines it all? And who *needs* to define what is real and what is not? Where does this idea come from?

Q: It comes from the mind...

K: Where did the mind come from? Don't blame the mind. You see, you already make up something. There's no mind, come on! The mind is just another idea. So, never mind. [Laughter] It's always nice, you say that the mind is guilty. It's the mind who did it, not me. [Laughter] I'm absolutely innocent but the mind did it. Fucking mind! I have to get rid of my mind, specially 'my' mind is too much for me. And *your* mind, I see you're totally from your mind. If your knowing comes from the heart – Whoah! then we're talking about the reality. [Laughter] But who makes this difference? Me!

Q [Another visitor]: Where does the mind come from?

K: How many times did I tell you that nothing comes? Ten years, I wasted my time. [Laughter] How many times did I talk about it? If I think about it, I get exhausted. But as your questions are inexhaustible, this answering machine is inexhaustible. All these questions, where and why... and I'm always, 'Why not'? Trying to destroy all these but I cannot destroy it as there's nothing to destroy. That's fun! It's just for sport. It's not expecting something to come out of it. This is just life living, knowledge knowing but there's no need of anything. There's no end to it.

Q: Hopeless!

K: That would be one hope too many. It's hopelessness. In

hopelessness there's no one who has or doesn't have hope because there's no ownership. But in no hope, there's still one who has no hope. For who? For 'me'. [Laughter] Hopelessness is like selflessness, existentialness... the Absolute realizing itself in hope and no hope, light and darkness, all of that. Two faces of what you are, two faces of Shiva – the light of Shiva and the darkness of Shiva. The no moon and the full moon. And in between there are all variations, fifty shades of grey of Shiva. [Laughter] Fifty, fifty, fifty, fifty billions and billions of experiences of this rainbow body of Shiva. There's extreme light and darkness and in between there's all rainbow body of what you are which is creating all colors and information and vibrations. [Pointing to a visitor] And she wants to get rid of it.

You create two poles, black and white... and in between there are all possibilities, because all is light in different vibrations creating all the rainbow – whatever it is, and that is your infinite body, your infinite realization as black and white. And in between all of that there's all this information and all these variations and all what can be imagined and not imagined. And I tell you, there's no end to it. Out of all of that there will always be a next moment of this rainbow body creating a unique flavor of this whatever, which comes from the absolute polarities of black and white –Wow! And you are That what is realizing itself as that. But only What you are is real but not the way you realize yourself – that's all.

Q [Another visitor]: Where does the relative arise from?

K: It doesn't arise, it's just one aspect of...

Q: But it arises from real, no?

K: It arises from that what is not relative.

Q: How can that be?

K: The form comes from the formless.

Q: But there's only one...

K: One is one too many.

Q: In this moment, our existence is as real as that what is existence...

K: That's what I just said. This moment in essence is totally Absolute, it's like a cake and this moment is like one slice of the Absolute cake.

Q: But it doesn't last...

K: No. Every slice lasts forever. This is the infinite now. This experience is as eternal as the essence of it. There's nothing to do.

Q: In the relative...

K: There's no relative in it, it's all Absolute.

Q: But there's some part of it that doesn't last...

K: There's an *experience* of relativity but that's not real.

Q: I'm saying, it is real for as long as it lasts...

K: Then it cannot be Reality because Reality cannot be sometimes there and sometimes not.

Q: But that's only after the now...

K: There's no 'after'.

Q: Everything is real in this moment...

K: You want to fix something that doesn't need to be fixed.

Q: When you speak it sounds like something needs to be fixed...

K: No. I just say nothing needs to be fixed because it's already fixed.

Q: The part of real that exists in this moment...

K: If you make it a part, it's already relative. You already start from relative creating something that's relative. The unreal creating unreal, that I always point to.

Q: But I'm saying it's not unreal...

K: But *I'm* saying it.

Q: Who's making the distinction?

K: I make it. And I'm sitting here. [Laughter] Otherwise people would not come to me. Consciousness would not listen to me if I would be saying...

Q: I didn't want to say that. [Laughter] I'm looking at the Buddhist analogy and the whole point of that is in relative there could be a pointer to the Absolute and I'm wondering how that analogy may have arisen. Is it not so that a frog could have jumped into an urn of milk and by moving around, it creates butter...

K: If you ask me, I agree that everything is possible. But then you can also say that if you pee in the ocean then the ocean gets enlightened.

Q: No it doesn't...

K: If everything is possible, even *that* is possible. If you pee in an ocean than the ocean gets enlightened. [Laughter] If that is right, then this is right too.

Q: If the frog jumps out of the urn...

K: Then there would be an enlightened frog. But who cares about an enlightened frog? [Laughter] It is possible. Even a French person can get enlightened! I never thought about that, but even *that's* possible! [Laughter] I agree with you, if that is possible then even when you spit in the ocean it may be gone. Everything's possible. Maybe a mosquito bites you and it gets enlightened. Everything's possible... but still there would be an enlightened mosquito and an ocean that's enlightened.

Q [Another visitor]: That's why they say that everything is Absolute...

K: The nature of the relative is Absolute but the Absolute is not relative. There's a little difference.

Q [Another visitor]: Yeah, the frog doesn't go back... [Laughter]

K: It's like Plato. The enlightened one has to go back to the cave because it's so fucking boring outside. So nothing is gained. Thank God there's no gaining in anything and no losing in anything - but yes you can have an experience of enlightenment. But what is gained by it? Are you different by being enlightened? I agree you can be enlightened, but who cares? Maybe your friends. I tell you when you get enlightened, for sure you have no friends anymore. [Laughter] That's the nature of enlightenment, there are no others. So you better stay unenlightened because only when you stay unenlightened you can have your relationships. Or so it seems like. But don't worry when you get enlightened, the next girl friend makes sure that you lose it again. [Laughter] What you gain you lose again, that for sure is how it all is.

Every understanding, every awakening that comes will be gone again, sooner or later it's gone. You may even hold it for ten lifetimes. There were fifteen lifetimes for Dalai Lama but one day Dalai Lama is gone. And even he's fed up being the Dalai Lama, he doesn't want to be reborn again. That's your primal fear that there's no end to that, one lifetime you're enlightened and the next not and you're already fed up of being enlightened.

Q [Another visitor]: So what if the enlightened one doesn't know that he's enlightened?

K: That's still one too many who doesn't know that he's not enlightened.

Q: So, there's no end?

K: There's no end. You just be that what has no beginning and no end, just be what you are.

Q: Then the Self becomes a joke, a cosmic drama...

K: It *is* a joke. Trying to attain yourself is a joke, for sure. This is an *ent*ertainment, not at*tain*ment.

Q: If the Lord or Parabrahman can extend the life...

K: If that one could extend the life, what kind of life would that be? Only a quantitative life.

Q: Absolutely no, because there's no end to the infinite anyway, there's no end to the Absolute. This is the idea of the masters that the whole universe is a Mandala of the divine...

K: And the end it's destroyed... shrppp[Making a rippling sound]. It's like the *mandalas* from the Buddhists, they make a very elaborate one and in one swish, they destroy it and just make another one.

Q: But for a moment there was something...

K: And then it's gone again. It's a joy of creation and the joy of destruction. The joy of creating and the joy of getting rid of it. Then you make place for a new one, a new *kaliyuga, yuga, yuga*. How many *yugas* are there?

Q: That doesn't gain anything or doesn't lose anything by that...

K: There's never more or less Life.

Q: That we can't know though because it could be constantly coming up with new life...

K: No. That's called relative life.

Q: How can the Absolute be relative?

K: How can there be a space at all in Absolute? How can there be distance in Absolute?

Q: There cannot be any...

K: If there's no such thing, then there can be no getting more or less in anything because there's not even a space for that to get more or bigger.

Q: Maybe there's a dimension...

K: But we're not talking about a maybe here. You can always say maybe there's a fifteenth dimension of the underworld of the fifth dynasty of puti-pati-tuki-tuki, there's something what is different. [Laughter] Yes, there will be differences, but does it make a difference? Would it make a difference for what you are or that what is the Self or Parabrahman? Would any way it's dreaming Itself make Parabrahman different? Or more or less? So, being Brahman not knowing Brahman is what you are and that cannot get anything out of anything.

Q: We would make our experience limited by logic or reasoning...

K: This is not reasoning, this is just being in the absence and in the presence, that's all.

Q: But the problem is...

K: You're always talking about the presence in which something happens, consciousness playing a game of presence. But this doesn't help anyone. The only experience of Happy-Nappy is that even in the Absolute absence of life, he is That what he is. And that what you are doesn't need any presence of life, that's the only thing what counts. The rest is fiction. All that is just brrmmmm... consciousness making waves of nothing. Only *that* is what counts, that your Absolute Nature does not depend on anything... and it never gets more or less by anything. There's nothing else which counts more. If you put all your energy and all your attention only to be that. By nature, you are that but not by putting any intellectual idea of the ninth dimension of whatever somewhere.

Just be that which is in spite of whatever and then if there's still someone who cares about it, let him care about it.

Q: To say that is like asking someone to stand on his own shoulders. You say that but it's impossible to do it...

K: I never asked you to do anything.

Q: You say be That...

K: But it's not a doing.

Q: But it is impossible...

K: It's impossible to *become* but it's even impossible *not* to *be*! You have to really make an effort *not* to be that, so just by being lazy, you are That, but not by any effort.

Q: By being lazy, you're just unhappy...

K: Who needs to be happy? [Laughter] Say it, who needs to be happy?

Group: Me!

Q: In the last talks of Nisargadatta Maharaj, he talks about being prior to consciousness. On what basis should we believe him? I know in Vedanta we have an idea about the man who can speak about the transcendental truth because he has no reason to deceive us...

K: You have to look for someone who has no advantage in listening to you.

Q: Yes, he has none for sure...

K: Look at me here. [Laughter]

Q: I just would like to say this to the group that all the funds that are given here in donation don't go to Karl but they support a charitable work for children...

K: But don't have pity with me otherwise you bring some home-knitted socks for me. [Laughter] Helplessness is joy. If I decide to sit or not to sit here, I would not enjoy that. I enjoy the helplessness that I cannot help to sit here... this is unavoidable. You cannot avoid yourself and this is the next what comes.

Q: But there's no resistance in that...

K: Without resistance it's like a river, not knowing where it ends.

Q: And that's okay...

K: It's not okay but it's just like a river. It's like Nisargadatta saying, 'On one end there's wisdom that tells me I'm nothing and on the other end there's love that tells me I'm everything... and in between my life flows'.

Q: How could he speak like that? Was it out of memory?

K: No, It's just being in spite of wisdom and in spite of love. Being in spite of whatever, that's life just flowing.

Q: But how can he speak from a place prior to consciousness?

K: How can you listen from the relative point? Everything is possible.

Q: Why?

K: You don't have to know why, it just happens.

Q: I don't know if a sage or a scripture has announced the final teachings like that...

K: In the tradition of Nisargadatta they talk like that, Dattatreya talked like that in Avadhuta Gita.

Q: It seemed he talked from there...

K: That's why it's said that rarely there's one in ages that speaks from there which is not a reference point.

Q: I'm just trying to insert an evolutionary nature to consciousness...

K: It's not evolutionary. It's like an accident sometimes someone talks from there. It's not by intention because that what is That, doesn't need that. It can talk from everywhere.

Q: What about mathematics when they talk about transmuted realities?

K: Zero-zero cannot be more than zero-zero.

Q: Not to us...

K: Zero zero zero zero.

Q: It's like two plus two is four in all possible worlds...

K: Whenever there's one, all the differences of various possible worlds arise. But from zero zero, nothing comes and into zero nothing goes.

Q: It's obviously not zero...

K: It's zero zero. You become the toilet of existence and you don't mind. [Laughter] You're this helplessness of a toilet and everyone can sit on you and goes away and the toilet cannot decide who sits on it. What comes next? Okay the next arse. [Laughter] The next arse wants to get rid of the shit as the previous arse wanted to get rid of the shit and you don't mind. That's not minding! You don't mind because there's helplessness because there are infinite arses sitting on you. [Laughter] And then you can call enlightenment as a flush because every once in a while you have a flash and then later everything goes away again. [Laughter] Just to draw a picture so that you can imagine it better.

This helplessness of this Absolute location which is Parabrahman, he cannot dream what he wants to dream because there's no one who can want something. Whatever can happen, will happen!

Q: Including what I said?

K: Whatever! Everything is possible, but it is also impossible *not* to be that. So, there's no way out of being That. No way out! But by being that, everything is possible. But the only thing what is impossible is that you can kill yourself... that you can know yourself in any way. So, everything is possible but the only thing that is not possible is knowing T hat what is everything.

Q: Everything is possible, even that...

K: That what knows everything cannot be known by Itself, because for that it needs two. That's called non-duality.

Q: If you say everything is possible, then there's chaos only. There's no redemption of any kind...

K: There's no hook you can be hooked from. If everything is possible, then okay, you can relax in peace.

Q: Except it's chaos...

K: Chaos and order come together but you're in order and in chaos That what you are. So, Peace cannot be disturbed by anything and the peace what can be disturbed by something is not Peace, it's just an absence of disturbance.

Q: This is a good argument for death...

K: Death cannot bring what you're looking for.

Q: You mentioned that this is what everyone longs for, to be nothing...

K: And I'm sitting here telling you that you'll not succeed in it.

Q: I know it's a hopeless attempt because every night we go to sleep and we wake up again...

K: You imagine that you woke up again like the day before, but you're not sure. You just hope not to wake up again. But then you wake up again and – shit!

Q: What is this attraction for emptiness?

K: It's longing to get out of discomfort. Longing to get out of misery, trying to end suffering, trying to end discomfort. And you think that absence of discomfort is better than the presence of discomfort.

Q: You think that the Source of consciousness is disturbed by consciousness?

K: No. You experience one who's disturbed by everything because he's even disturbed that he exists.

Q: So, we cannot know what gave rise to it...

K: There's no guilt in it.

Q: So, Shiv is okay with himself...

K: There's no one who needs to be okay, that's the problem. That what you are doesn't need anything and that what you experience always needs something. Consciousness always needs something.

Q: The next experience...

K: Whatever. There will always be the next, never satisfied. There's no satisfaction in consciousness. This is an experience of consciousness as a discomfort, because every experience is separation and separation is discomfort.

Q: The odd thing is if you figure it out, it doesn't help you at all. Even if you understand it at the Absolute level, on the relative level it doesn't help at all...

K: And I'm sitting here and telling you be happy that you'll never succeed and no one ever before you got it. No one ever before you made it, including Ramana or Buddha or Christ. That's why I like Buddha. His pointer was – I'm the Absolute failure and by that I am what I am. I am what I am because I failed to know myself. So, I failed even in failing. I cannot even fail. So, I even failed to know or to be what I am. I failed not to be what I am! I failed in all ways and by that, I am That which always fails.

Q [Another visitor]: The way of the Buddha is difficult because he gave rise to a flower...

K: Out of the locus comes the lotus. Being the absolute failure, you realize yourself. Locus is the toilet, being the toilet of everything. Out of that toilet you are, the lotus arises. You realize yourself from that what you are – as whatever – but not as That what you are. You're already that what is Reality realizing itself! Being That what is Buddha or Parabrahman dreaming himself but is never part of the dream. You failed to know yourself, to find yourself in the dream. And failing absolutely is Nisargadatta's ultimate medicine – being that what was never sick and never needs to be healed by anyone because your reality cannot be more real than it is.

Q: So the relative can only be a pointer, it can never be a substitute to that what it is...

K: There can be pointers in the relative to that what is not relative, but the pointers are not true. They can only point to it like the finger that points to the moon. The good company that Ramana talks about is that you're in the presence of That which doesn't allow any – whatever. Now you think you're a bull fighter and you have to tame the bull but that's bullshit, because what you are never needs to be tamed by anyone. And that mind what needs to be tamed is still one mind too many. So, never mind.

Being the presence points you to the bullshit you're trying to do. You're a *torero* who thinks there's a *Toro*. There's a bull and you're the fighter and you fight to tame that bull because you want to have peace. But you fail to tame the bull because the bull cannot be tamed. For a moment you think that you tamed the bull but then it wakes up as something else. So what to do? The infinite bullfight. So it's all bullshit.

Q [Another visitor]: Sadhana is to listen to this?

K: Ramana called this the highest tapas. The highest *tapa* is to listen to what you are from That what you are. What to do? If you put all your energy of trying to end misery and suffering to that what you are, you'd instantly be That what you are.

Q: That's the most hopeful thing you've said in a long time...

K: I mean it. If you put all your attention, all the energy that is now trying to be happy, all that energy you waste on this idea of happiness... if you put all that energy to that what you are, instantly you'd be that what you are. I agree with them – totally. You're just wasting all your attention on shit. But what can you do? You give all your attention to fleeting shadows of you. And even the light is a fleeting shadow. So put all your attention to that what you are.

Q: You can put lipstick on a pig but it's still a pig... [Laughter]

Q [Another visitor]: It sounds like we should just go in a cave...

K: That's not what was meant. In the cave, you give attention to the absence. You always give the attention to some location, to some presence or absence, so even the absence is not it. You should give attention to that what is attention and not to any presence or absence. The absence doesn't bring it and the presence doesn't bring it. The absence is as false as the presence.

Q [Another visitor]: But it's closer to it than the presence?

K: There's no 'close' to it. Otherwise you're in the absence closet. Both are false. It's empty.

Q: What about this one? [Pointing to an imaginary point on the forehead]

K: It's empty, it's just the third eye.

Q: Meditating on the absence rather than...

K: No. You just look into the absence and by not finding yourself in the absence or presence, maybe then it's okay.

Q: It's not closer?

K: Nothing is closer or further away from what you are because you are what you are in the Absolute distance, in the Infinite and here.

Q: In Nisargadatta's last teachings, why did he talk about *prana*?

K: *Prana* is your divine body. You are the divine itself and *prana* is your divine body – that's Shiva and Shakti.

Q: But there's no form for prana...

K: You eat yourself all the time, that's prana. When you eat yourself, you don't have to digest it.

Q: You said something else last time...

K: Now I say something else. [Laughter] Why should I remember the bullshit from whenever? This is the divine [Opening his hands outwards] and this [Pointing to the body] is your divine body and you eat yourself. And the beauty of that is you don't have to digest anything. There's no need of digestion. When you eat yourself you don't have to digest yourself. But everything else needs some effort of digesting it. And what comes out of digestion? Shit. That's why it's called a shit body. It's a shit factory. But when you are what you are you just experience yourself. That's called Self experience – being that what's experiencing itself as being Reality and the realization of it. In nature there's no difference. So, you're life living life. You are life living or living life, because in nature there's no difference. You're living yourself in living and in not living... in presence and in absence. The absence doesn't make you less and the presence doesn't make you more. That's what Nisargadatta said about wisdom and love – the wisdom of absence and the love of everything. But both cannot make you more or less as you are, so enjoy yourself in each of them. Enjoy yourself as that what is That. And that joy doesn't have to digest itself. But everything else, trying to get something out of it [Exhaling deeply] is a reader's digest.

Q [Another visitor]: Can I put attention to the unknowingness?

K: No, even that's too much. You should not put attention in anything other than that what is attention itself. In putting attention to attention, that one who has attention disappears. And in the absence of that, you are that what is the presence or the absence of that one. Without That what is what you are, you are neither presence or absence. Put total attention to That what is in spite of presence or absence, and not putting attention to the knowing or the not knowing. Whatever you put attention to is not what you are. Put attention to that what *is* attention! Be the seer and not that what can be seen, that is putting attention to the Absolute Seer which never can be seen in anything, neither presence or absence, and not putting attention to what-is is yet another idea. Put attention to that what is not an idea and not any concept and that is That what you are.

You *were* That, you *are* That and you *will* be That! So, it's not something that comes or goes. It was already there, it is and it will be. So, it's not something you have to care about or you have to put in your pocket or something, or you need to remember. That what was, is and will be, is That what you are. There's an effortlessness of being That. So, put attention only to That and not this hard work slavery of trying to get enlightened. I would not say that you're already enlightened because it's the same bullshit.

Q [Another visitor]: I just did it...

K: What did you?

Q: I just put attention to attention...

K: It is not a doing. If you did it, it was one doer too many.

Q: Of course...

K: You are always off course. [Mocking] I just put attention to attention and look at me, I'm still here. [Laughter]

Q: That's where grace comes in...

K: Nothing comes in! [Laughter] The saints are marching in and the grace comes in and you say – Hello grace, what took you so long? [Laughter] I was waiting so long for you, you fucking arsehole, why didn't you come earlier? Mama mia... I had opened all the doors for you and I was so much in Vipasanna training. Fuck off grace I don't need you anymore!

Q: I've got attention...

K: You have an intention of getting something by putting attention to attention. That's intention, not attention. Now you know the difference between attention and intention. Does it help you? You only talk about intention and not attention.

Q [Another visitor]: What is the difference between the impersonal and personal?

K: Both are bullshit – personal shit and impersonal shit.

Q: You're pointing to that what is beyond personal and impersonal?

K: I'm not pointing anywhere.

Q: And I cannot make anything out of it either?

K: No. Because what you make out of it will be shit only. Whatever comes out of something, what is that? Sat-shit-ananda. [Laughter] And you can only experience yourself in shit. You can never experience *chit* – impossible. Knowledge cannot experience Knowledge. Whatever you experience is ignorance but it doesn't make you ignorant. So, what's the problem? Where is the danger for you? What is there to do? If the experience of existence doesn't make you *exist*, what's the problem? You are in existence and in non-existence that what you are. And That what you are doesn't even need to *exist* to exist! So, what's the problem if existence gets wider or bigger, some enlightened one or realized one. What is all of that? Just a big entertainment show you cannot avoid – that's all.

So, be entertained by what you are because you cannot stop the program and you don't have the remote control to change the program. What can you do? And you have to experience yourself in every possible and impossible way anyway. Whatever can happen, will happen, already happened, because whatever is possible is possible... if it *can* happen it will happen! So, it *already* happened.

Q [Another visitor]: Nothing happens...

K: That's one nothing too many. Even shit happens in nothing. But I know nothing happens. Nothing ever happened sounds good too. No, you have to make it a paradox – In all the happenings nothing ever happens. But if you say nothing happens, it's still one happening too many. Otherwise it becomes another title for an esoteric book – that's all.

[Looking at the clock]

Oh we still have time. We can make consciousness enlightened for thousands of times in that time and still nothing will happen. [Laughter] How many times did consciousness became cosmic consciousness and went back to the relative consciousness? How many times did it travel from the relative one to the big one? Like in Buddhism the little vehicle going up and down and nothing ever happened. Did that what you are find rest in cosmic consciousness? You have to experience yourself in the restless and in the rest. And That what you are doesn't need any rest. And you cannot rest in anything, not even in yourself... because even yourself is an idea.

What you are doesn't need to rest and that what needs to rest is... what? An experience of an infinite traveler called consciousness which is looking at all the possibilities of consciousness and can never find any end to it, as there's no end to the light of Shiva – neither in the inside or outside. And whoever claims that he found his true nature is for sure a liar. Anyone here who knows his true nature? Yesterday there was one. [Laughter]

Q [Another visitor]: He was very nasty...

K: Just for the difference, because you are so nasty. [Laughter] He brought joy to everyone because everyone was happy that it was not him. [Laughter] The day before I said that bad people make everyone else feel good, it's the good persons that you have to worry about.

Q [Another visitor]: Doesn't the longing need to be a hundred percent even if it leads to a hundred percent failure?

K: Hundred percent is still not enough.

Q: It seems like all the great ones like Buddha were hundred percent into knowing what is suffering...

K: And he failed.

Q: He failed a hundred percent but it started with such an incredible need. I think most of us are like ten percent or five percent...

K: As I said yesterday, one month in high season here and the rest in McDonalds again. [Laughter] And that's grace, no one can decide if you give attention to That. Ramana said you have to be like ten meters under water that you cannot breathe anymore... only then you are interested in that what you are. Otherwise if this dream is still okay, you can manage, then you're not interested. So, by grace there will be a depression, a total vacuum that nothing makes sense anymore. All of that is so empty. The wisdom of emptiness is eating you up, you are not looking for it.

When Self is after elf, it creates that void, because nothing is interesting anymore. Only when Self is involved and interested in Itself, this happens. Otherwise it's just crash test dummies having another Mercedes or another awakening experience from the Vipasanna training. All of that is like having a new Mercedes and telling your friends about how many *satoris* you had and counting your little absences – I went to absence today at least five times. [Laughter] Let's talk about it. You'd like to sit with a fire around your cave and would like to talk about it. My first teacher was a Zen master and the second was that. This gave me that experience and I learnt something from the second one. Even if you're interested in spiritual or esoteric stuff, it's just what it is. And that cannot be done by anyone.

Q: But there has to be a need...

K: The need is just a side effect produced because the Self is after the self. If the Self is only after the self, there will be side effects that the need and the depression and the void appears. But not *because* of the void the Self is after the self... you always turn it around.

Because the Self already has the interest for itself the side effects happen, but not because of the side effects you're looking for the Self. Already the Self is looking for the Self and that creates side effects, that you go to places like these. But not because you go to places like these, you're interested in the Self. That's the tiger's mouth, the tiger already has you. The Self already is That what can be satisfied only by being the Self. You don't have to worry, just trust that. Everything is already done. That's what is meant when they say that when the tiger gets you, it doesn't leave you alone anymore. It will always be around you. [Laughter] It bites you as much as it is needed and it gives you circumstances which are needed, but not by any circumstance you are interested in the Self. It creates that what is needed.

Have faith in That alone which is the inner guru, which is what you are. I'm not interested in making disciples. I'm talking to the guru and Ramana says only by lighting of What-you-are... that fire alone burns you out by its own way... depending on your karmic whatever. But it will burn you away. But the only thing that's needed is that the fire has to be there. That the fire is burning for your Self alone... and that cannot come by anything. That's why I talk directly to the fire, lighting the fire alone, giving interest only to that. That's called a Sadguru. By speaking, by looking, by touch, whatever is needed - or by silence. Okay, I agree that the highest is Silence, but if that doesn't work then you need some words, hitting whatever needs to be hit. That's why I talk.

And when I say that I talk to Myself, I mean it. And only by talking to myself, whatever I say is hitting... because whatever I talk to, I'm already there, and not by convincing you or making you believe in what I say. I have no interest in that. I don't need believers. I don't want to create a new religion. Ramana didn't want to create a new religion but now it becomes Ramanaism – like Christ never wanted to create Christianity or Buddha was never interested in Buddhism. But later on, the devil takes care about what you said. [Laughter] The devil says 'You do your job and I'll take care of the business.' [Laughter] But why not? It's always the same. The successors make a family business.

Q: When I was with Nisargadatta Maharaj and later with Ranjit Maharaj, the flavours that they were pointing to were very different. Nisargadatta was just fire and Ranjit was more love. Why this difference?

K: It was just a different expression of love. The character is different so the tool is different. But That what is expressing itself is not different.

Q: With Ranjit the quality of that was more like love, I can never call it love being with Nisargadatta...

K: When I look at Nisargadatta it's pure love. Destroying all your concepts, that's love. That's Shiva in action. Ranjit was just a bachelor who never had a wife at home. [Laughter] He was never married so he could be sweet. I met Ranjit but I know Nisargadatta by heart too. That what was talking through them is not different.

Q: It was the same...

K: It was just Self expressing itself and talking to itself in different ways. I talk to everyone differently. To some I'm very harsh and to some I'm very soft. It's always different but it is always as it has to be. I never have any doubt what comes out of here. If something counts at all, then it's that doubtlessness and carelessness alone, and not like a chicken who wants to embrace his little tra la la...

So maybe he spoke to you in that way because maybe there was a resonance in that way and to someone else totally differently. I always wonder why I'm so different all the time. Sometimes I even talk like Karl. [Laughter] I never doubt what comes. In the essence it's the doubtlessness or the certainty of That, that's all.

It's this unshakeable certainty. The presence of this unshakeable certainty which he presented, no one could disturb what he was. This certainty of doubtlessness of being What you are, that's all. The rest is just – whatever – pointing to something.

Q: Don't those differences show a bridge between the Absolute and the relative...

K: What you see expresses itself differently but it's not different in Nature. This is not a bridge, this is self-realization as That. That what expresses itself differently is not different in nature. It's not a bridge, it's like a recognition. It's like recognizing that what is living here and there is not different. It's just a different loudspeaker, a different way of expression... it's not a bridge. You see there are differences, but they don't *make* any difference... that's all! But it's quite something to see so many expressions, so many differences, these infinite rainbow vibrations, but there are no differences. Maybe you see that there is no bridge needed? *That's* the bridge! You have to cross the bridge which is not there. What to do?

I can't say because I didn't go to so many teachers, no interest. When I went to Bombay, there was only a successor (Ramesh Balsekar) and Ranjit.

Q [Another visitor]: Who was Ranjit?

K: A co-disciple of Nisargadatta who lived for twenty five years longer. He started talking when Nisargadatta died.

Q: Did he live in Bombay?

K: Maybe not living in Bombay but you could find him in Bombay. [Laughter]

Q [Another visitor]: In a tiny room...

K: Now everyone compares me to him and says he was always available in a tiny room and why are you not like him, I say fuck you. There was one Ranjit and it was already too many. Then they make a standard again and people think that now you have to be like him. Then they compare with their beloved Guruji and if the other one is not exactly the same then it's not right.

It's like your girlfriend dies and you want to find the next one who should be exactly the same because you had such good sex with her and it was always fine. She never bothered you and you never had to do the dishes like your mother. Every man looks for another mother because mother never made the dishes without complaining. [Laughter] The love was without limits and now you want a girl friend like that and that's impossible. You will always be disappointed.

How to end comparison? It's impossible. You will always compare again. There will be comparing, comparing.

Q: The question I had was not out of comparing...

K: No. But I meet many Osho widows and UG widows. If I don't say enough shit in one day then they say UG was saying much more shit.

Q: What I wanted to say was both of them truly believed in their Sadguru...

K: Or didn't believe in their guru. They left the belief system of the guru because they recognized themselves in their guru. So, the guru died and they died. So, they didn't believe in the guru or the word of the guru... they just started to recognize themselves in their guru. If you recognize yourself in the guru, you and the guru is gone.

Q: But if you recognize yourself in the guru shows that the guru...

K: No. That can be a chicken too. Life doesn't have to be a guy in white that you imagine like a guru. Life is your guru. It can be your kid, your mother, even your husband. [Laughter] One should not limit it to the figure of the love or teacher in an ashram. There's no special place for it. You are permanently surrounded by what you are. You swim in yourself. And the Self can be in every fish you meet as your guru. Even the smallest thing can explode in you. It doesn't need to be Nisargadatta or Ranjit. Otherwise it would depend again.

Everything is possible in any moment. Every word I say may hit you – or not. It can always be a key experience and this key experience opens that what was already open. This paradox is amazing. It opens That what's already open. You don't need to say – Open Sesame. Whatever you try to do to open it, you close it again. Just be lazy.

Q [Another visitor]: Can I say something?

K: No. [Laughter] I mean you cannot say something but if what you are wants something, it would.

Q: Nisargadatta said that you worship the consciousness as your guru and it is nothing but the feeling of I Amness...

K: That was in I Am That in the beginning. Everyone talks in the beginning like that. He makes standards too and then later on he said it was all bullshit. You can only trust a guru you cannot trust. [Laughter] It's very profound. You can only trust a guru that you cannot trust what he says next. If you find a guru that repeats himself permanently, you should just run away. You should trust a guru that you cannot trust what comes next from him. You have to be in the wonder of what comes next and he destroys what he said the day before. I like all of that with Nisargadatta. He lied as much as he could lie and then he destroyed all the lies the next day. Forget him, you never met him. Don't repeat what you have heard and what you've read. It's all bullshit.

Q: This is contradicting...

K: You have to be with one who contradicts in life and not in books. That's what Ranjit permanently said, don't read the books of dead gurus, as there are not even living ones, because the guru that's alive is not a guru. You have to find a dead guru, I mean it. I point to that, you have to find a dead guru and not a guru who's alive, who is trying to pierce you like a bull. You have to find a dead guru who doesn't want anything from you.

Q [Another visitor]: And what about you?

K: I'm neither dead or alive. Now she wants to put me in a trap – What kind of guru are you? [Laughter] These are the reasons why girlfriends are made.

A dead guru means whatever that is, it has absolutely no interest in you. About how you are, if you get something, if you understand something or not. This carelessness – come on! That's what you're longing for. This carelessness cannot be given and cannot be transmitted. But you have to find one who's not there... but the one who's not there is too much, even *that* one.

I like Ramana. Everyone came to him and told him, this has to be like this and then he just asked, who makes a standard? Who knows how it has to be? Does it have to be a dead one or an alive one? Maybe both are concepts. All what we can say about a guru is a concept and doesn't fit at all. Because guru is the Self and the Self can never be defined by any one.

I can make a teaching and sound very profound and explain it. But it would be as much bullshit as anyone else said before. But what to do?

Q [Another visitor]: What do you do for the rest of the day?

K: Thinking about your bloody questions. [Laughter]

Q: I'm just curious...

K: And that's stupid. Being curious is stupid you know that, because it kills you. When you are curious to be what you are, you are already not what you are.

17th Feb 2016
Tiruvannamalai

Chapter Five

The Intellect Is An Infinite Grave Of Dead Concepts

～

K: Welcome to the alien-nation! [Laughter]

Q: Is it the golden awareness that creates this show?

K: No. The golden awareness is already created.

Q: Does it experience the show?

K: No. It's the experience of gold, but the experience of gold is already a part of the creation, it's already an imaginary gold. In that total imagination, maybe gold is superior imagination... but it is still an imagination. It's like the auro-bingo – the super consciousness... but it's still an imagination. It's the best you can get but even the best is not good enough.

Q: But the one who thinks he can do something, has to make an effort...

K: It is the best you can do in the dream, finding the golden awareness, a notion of pure presence. It's the best you can do, but it's not good enough because it's still a 'maybe'. If that would be

PEACE OFF: AND BE WHAT YOU ARE

your real nature, your experience should be uninterrupted. Where is this golden awareness in deep-deep sleep? What would you say?

Q: I don't know...

K: You see. In deep-deep sleep you don't know any gold or anyone who calls anything gold. But now in presence there is gold, silver, rainbow – all part of this realization and all part of this presence. But the presence is the presence, but you are with and without the presence – what to do? You cannot find your natural state in this presence. Your natural state is never part of anything.

Q: Mike Tyson says everyone's got a plan 'till they're punched in their face...

K: Yes. It's like everyone is enlightened until he gets a new girlfriend – the next punch in the face. No. What you can get in this dream you have to leave again, you know that. You have to look for that which cannot get lost and you cannot gain. You have to look for that what you cannot forget, what you don't need to remember. That you have to meditate upon, you have to put your attention only to that which is not depending on any special state.

But if you ask me that if you want a nice life in this presence, then awareness or the witness state is not so bad. So yes, in the dream it is the best you can get. If you want to have a pleasant dream, go for it! But maybe it will not satisfy you. For sure, it will not satisfy you.

Q [Another visitor]: The idea that you can only be what you cannot *not* be...

K: It's a pointer.

Q: This is something you understood at the age of thirteen?

K: It came to me in San Diego. In the first talk in Carlsbad in California, there was a guy who read Ramana and said whenever I try to be as I am, I lose it. I replied then you go one step further, be what you cannot *not* be. Then he was quiet. You cannot make a concept out of it. It was like a koan. It breaks your ownership in one instant. What you cannot *not* be, you cannot occupy by ideas or by concepts. In that sense it's like a koan. And for sure later you make a concept again... you try very hard. But for one instant maybe there's an absence of any idea of what you are and what you are not, because this you cannot grasp. It's not for your intellect. It's not what can be understood or needs to be understood. It doesn't depend on understanding. It's absolutely independent of one who understands or knows or doesn't know. Just being that what you cannot not be. In that you rest because this is effortlessness. That what is living by effort, the doer or the non-doer, cannot remain there. So, there's an absolute non-doership in it... or not even an idea of existence. This came to me, I didn't invent it. But it fits and that's why I repeat it.

Q: When did you start giving talks?

K: In Berlin in 2000 but before that I used to sit in Tiruvannamalai in German Bakery and then some organizers came and said we can organize you. I said – Fuck you! My organs are nice enough. [Laughter] I resisted for some time and as I said the bladder went full and I couldn't sleep anymore and there was a pressure and I said let's try it once. Then it started. The first night there were four people. In the second night no one came. [Laughter] And I was happy and laughing at the organizers and I said if tomorrow no one comes, that's it. It was like a burden was released. This is not for me, thank God and praise the Lord – just in case. And then the next night, twelve people, fuck! And then it starts...

It's like if you have a full bladder then you have to pee. It's like a joy of peeing because something is full. It's like when you are gifted by that, you have to perform. If you don't perform then you cannot sleep because the energy just keeps you awake all the time. That's the only reason I sit here, so that I can sleep. I don't sit here for someone else. This is very selfish. For sure I don't have any idea that I'm a Messiah and I need to save the world from something. And I know I cannot help you anyway because what you are doesn't need to be helped, and what I try to help is a hopeless case anyway. [Laughter]

This is for fun. It's because you have to pee (be) where you are. When you are That, you have to pee. So, pee as you are. [Laughter]

Q: But you were never a disciple of anyone?

K: My father tried. And I always looked at him and asked, 'Who are you?' and he got very angry. He wanted to convince me that I'm his son. Ha ha ha... try harder. [Laughter] My mother nearly succeeded. I was saved because she was the most complaining lady on earth. I had to run away because I could not listen anymore. I was blessed by a father who didn't make me a son and a mother who complained me away. [Laughter]

Q [Another visitor]: Do you have brothers and sisters?

K: [Pointing to the previous visitor] Are you both working together today? [Laughter] He's the psychotherapist and she's the patient, sitting in Goa and working out a new therapy.

Q: Did you read books?

K: Yes, mainly Gala. It's a German yellow press magazine. When I was a child I read Mickey Mouse, Batman, Superman. I was fascinated by Krypton. [Laughter]

Q: Were you fascinated by Ramesh Balsekar?

K: Never. I just went there only because I read Nisargadatta six weeks earlier. I read 'I Am That' and in the German edition it mentioned that there's a guy sitting in Bombay and is his successor. I just came to India to see who's the successor of Nisargadatta. After three days, I was not so convinced. He always pointed to Arunachala and Ramana as his biggest influence. I said then I better go there and not sit here in the 'working and thinking mind' situation. [Laughter] I was instantly bored, it was fantastic. It was like my mother, he bored me away by concepts. And so many psychotherapists came there, trying to rape the mind and trying to make something good out of the mind. Thinking mind is bad and working mind is good. I had that experience yesterday – Was that working mind or thinking mind? And Ramesh answers very patiently, 'It was in between. [Laughter] But you are on the way, understanding will happen'.

I liked him. I adored that he was so patient with all these psychotherapists. I would've killed them right away. The most intelligent bastards from America, the psychotherapists. That's why they're called shrinks because they want to make you little. They want to shrink you. They make you little because they tell you what's wrong with you and why you need some therapy. I hated them in the beginning already. And Ramesh sat there and was being very patient with those criminals called shrinks. They're worse than lawyers and lawyers are already the worst case scenario, but shrinks you should kill at the first sight – decompose them. Any shrink here? [Laughter]

Q: Did you have any desire to meet Osho?

K: I had enough girl friends at home. [Laughter] That trick never worked with me – free sex. I had that back home, why should I go to Osho? I looked quite handsome when I was young. [Laughter] And all the people I know that went to Osho – no. And then having sex with them? No! [Laughter] Come on, I have taste.

Anything else I should've done?

Q [Another visitor]: Were you ever into black *tantra*?

K: Me? No. I read Aleister Crowley because the gallerist from Berlin was in that community and he wanted me to read it first before I can have an exhibition there. And he asked me, 'Are you ready for that?' I said no. [Laughter] Again, I was saved by taste because in black *tantra* you have to fuck with everybody. You have to find the most ugly, old, whatever. And you have to do things you would've never done and the idea is that if you overcome your disgust, you overcome your ego. You get rid of your ego because you have no taste anymore. [Laughter] That's black *tantra*, sleeping with corpses. You want to do that? Are you attracted to that? That's why you're with him? [Pointing to the partner] [Laughter]

I hate the white *tantra* as I hate the black *tantra*. The esoteric white *tantra* is just as worse. In Germany Hitler was a black *tantrik*. They brought the Lamas from Tibet and asked them to give bad dreams to the leaders of the West. This trying to rule the world and all these esoteric, fascistic, nazzism. I was never attracted to that. Again, I was saved by taste.

Q: You were nine years without having sex...

K: That was something that happened, I didn't do it. Why are you so interested in my past? Do you want to write my biography? Everyone wants to make this standard, why is he sitting there and I'm sitting here? Why him and why not me? Everyone wants to find the secret.

Q [Another visitor]: I think the secret is that we're all special and you are not...

K: I'm very special. [Laughter] Again, you see!

Q: How do we get rid of trying to be special?

K: By being special. Who gives a fuck if you're special or not? Do you think existence needs you not to be special to be what it is? Do you really think that existence cares if you're special or not? Come on! You can be special as hell and no one cares.

Q: Then I'm not very special...

K: That's really special now.

Q [Another visitor]: What is the difference between 'Who Am I' and this...

K: It's just different approaches.

Q: But basically it's the same?

K: No. Basically it's all bullshit.

Q: So, what's the difference?

K: There's no difference. It's all bullshit. She wants me to elaborate between this and that. I'm not here to work, come on!

Q [Another visitor]: So, you'd rather play with us? [Laughter]

K: No. Every woman has a shrink inside.

Q [Another visitor]: Does the Absolute need energy?

K: Yes. What a question. Whatever you make out the Absolute needs or doesn't need, whatever I'd say would be wrong anyway.

Everyone is interested in Karl today and not in what I am. It's amazing, I'm never interested in this Karl anymore, but since I'm not interested everyone else is interested in Karl. It's like since my mother died everyone wants to be my mother.

Q [Another visitor]: What is the difference between sleep and deep-deep sleep?

K: For three months I talk to this guy... it's really like spitting into a septic tank. [Laughter]

Q: Is it possible to be aware in deep sleep?

K: Yes.

Q: And in deep-deep sleep?

K: No. Deep-deep sleep is the absence of... absence-presence, awareness or not-awareness of whatever one knows or doesn't know. That's the absence of any presence *or* absence. That's the nature of deep-deep sleep.

Q [Another visitor]: Is the deep-deep sleep same as the Absolute?

K: No. Then it would be different to something else. No. You're in deep-deep sleep in the absence of any presence of anyone who knows or doesn't know what one is and what one is not, you are. That's all. The Absolute doesn't need any presence to exist – or absence!... as you're in the presence and absence that what you are. That's the pointer of deep-deep sleep and not that you are the deep-deep sleep. You are what you are in deep-deep sleep and you are now what you are. So, the deep-deep sleep and the presence or absence doesn't make any difference for you. Whatever happens in the presence doesn't make you more or less. The absence cannot kill you and the presence cannot make you more alive. You are that Life that never needs to live or to die. In the experience of death you are the same as in the experience of life. But you are neither life or death – that's all. I just repeat that all the time. The one and only pointer. And only by being That what is absolutely independent of any presence or absence of whatever you can imagine or not, you cannot get more or less by any imaginary experience of any kind. But you have to imagine yourself, you have to dream yourself if you like it or not.

So, you have to realize yourself. But not by your realization you get more real, or unreal. You are already That what is realizing itself and by that realization it cannot get more or less as you are. But you have to realize yourself.

Q: When you are in a coma?

K: There's no 'one' in coma.

Q: In deep-deep sleep...

K: Yes. You can call that as coma and now it's *amok*. [Laughter] The Greeks are quite correct. This is amok and the absence is coma., but coma is *amok*, and *amok* is coma... The experience of *amok* is this presence or the form, and coma is the absence or the formless... the information and the non-form. But you are in the *amok* and in the coma as awareness. But even that is not what you are.

Q: In deep-deep sleep there's still consciousness?

K: There has to be an existence that there can be a deep-deep sleep. Without existence there would be not even the absence of existence. The Absolute existence is even in the absence of existence That what it is. So, it doesn't have to exist to exist. And that what has to exist to exist, you can call a phantom existence, a depending existence, in that What you are. And that is fact that you are as you are in the absence That. That is called sat-is-faction and not sat-is-*fiction* in the presence thing.

All what you experience here is fiction. And then out of the fiction you want to make a fact. But you cannot because whatever fiction that you can find, any concept, you can doubt again. So you land in any fiction and you depart again. And part of the fiction is this world, then the spirit and then the father... all three are fiction. And that's why in Jesus' case it was called cruci-fiction because the body was gone, the spirit was gone and even the father on the cross was gone. He said even the father has forsaken me. But maybe he was happy that even the father was fake. He just realized on the cross that the body is false, the spirit is false and the father is false and What he is doesn't need anything. The whole Trinity, the whole family, was actually Jesus' family constipation session. [Laughter]

This is really the nature of family constellation or constipation – that you believe that you are the son of a father, but all of that in a way is cruci-fiction because nothing happened in it. It was all fiction, from the beginning. So, that realization of Jesus who became Christ already started as a cruci-fiction because nothing happened to what he was. No body, no spirit, no father – bye, bye. And still I Am what I Am. Then he entered the land of the dead or the absence and still he existed. From there no one came back because then he realized himself as the father, the spirit and the son... but he's *not* the father, *not* the spirit and *not* the son. But you cannot get rid of your family, that's the problem.

Q [Another visitor]: He came back but That was already there...

K: That's what I meant. By the spear piercing his heart, the body was gone, the spirit was gone. He asked the father why have you forsaken me? I would have said, thank God now even the father is gone. Who needs you anyway? Who was there?

You cannot leave What you are, so he didn't come back. When he started to realize himself from the Christ consciousness, which is Shiva, you can say... Shiva had to realize himself as the father, spirit and the son whether he likes it or not. He had to realize itself: that's the pointer, that there's no way out.

Q: The other pointer could be that you don't leave either the horizontal one or the vertical one...

K: You have to carry your cross. That's the meaning of it. The cross is the symbol of the vertical spirit, the horizontal world and the centre which is awareness. This is the cross you have to carry. You cannot get rid of your cross, that's another pointer. The vertical spirit, the horizontal matter and the centre of it which is awareness. You have to carry your cross, you cannot get rid of your cross. You are crucified to what you are. You cannot leave what you *are* and that's the nature of crucifixion. You cannot leave what you *are* because you *are* the horizontal, you *are* the vertical and you *are* the centre of it. But you *are* not the vertical which is different from the horizontal or the center of it. You *are* That which is the cross. And by *being* the cross you don't have to carry it.

Q: You cannot leave it...

K: You cannot leave what you are because you *are* the cross.

Q: So, there's nobody coming back from it...

K: But he's not coming back by coming back.

Q: So, how does the resurrection fit in?

K: One part of what you are is the absence. You are complete in the absence and in the presence. Both have to be there. But now in case of the seekers, absence is missing. Like Ramana having the death experiencing is experiencing the absence of life and he is still what he is. Then it becomes like no way out, because if you cannot even escape from the absence, then there's no way out of the presence or the absence, as you are That. So, no way out in any sense *or* non-sense.

Q: But you are not even at home in the Absolute?

K: There's no home for you because there's no need for one. The home is that you don't need one. The freedom is that you don't need freedom. You're free from freedom, you're free from home, you're free from knowledge. When they asked Ramana, where would you go when you die? Ramana said where could I go? I am That. What I Am never comes and never goes. From what? Who came and who goes? Only ghosts come and go. That's why they're called go-sts.

Q: From that point, there's no time, no change...

K: There's an experience of time but it doesn't make time, as there's an *experience* of separation but it doesn't separate anything. I agree that there's an experience of it but it doesn't make it reality. I don't deny the experience of separation.

Q: This attraction from one state to the other, the relative to the absolute and the other way round. This cruci-fiction is taking place in all levels. When you wake up in the morning, there's already an attraction towards the self. We don't have a choice about which one of the selves we identify ourselves with...

K: You love everything actually, even hating is loving. There's no moment without love.

Q: In the same way at the end of the day we can't help being attracted towards the absence before we fall asleep...

K: You can say this is just the way you realize yourself. There's no 'me' who is attracted or not. This is just Reality realizing itself. This is just the way of realizing yourself as a personal 'me'.

Q: But the Absolute itself is attracted to the relative...

K: There's no attraction possible because there's no two. The Self is never attracted to anything. It is experiencing itself as one that is attracted to something.

Q: Why does that happen?

K: Why not?

Q: You say that about the Absolute on what basis? If it is as you are saying, none of this would appear...

K: There's no why. Why not? How many times did I tell you that the Reality has to realize itself, there's no difference. It's not Absolute being attracted to it.

Q: Why should it realize itself if there's no attraction?

K: There's no why in it.

Q: You always talk about the tendency of love. When I talk about attraction, you say it does not...

K: I don't say it's attracted to itself, I say it is loving itself. It's not because of an attraction but you want to make it an attraction. I say there's no attraction. It doesn't need attraction to love. It's unconditional and you try to make it conditional, that's what I fight.

Q: I say it's not conditional...

K: But you say it's attracted to it.

Q: The Absolute cannot help itself, otherwise why is it doing it?

K: Why do you contradict yourself now? I'm here to contradict myself, not you. [Laughter]

Q: I just make it like a dog chasing its own tail...

K: You are chasing your own tail, you know that, that's a fairy tale. That's why everything is fair because it's a fairy tale. [Laughter]

Q: No problem, but still. [Laughter] The Brahmasutra says how do you explain the manifestation is a big question...

K: The beauty of your nature is that it doesn't need to explain itself to be itself. And to be that what you are it doesn't need any explanation and that what now tries to explain it or tries to find something is a futile attempt of an intellect which tries to know intellect.

Q: You got me there. This is just for fun... [Laughter] I like to fail. I enjoy failing in public with you. It's a pleasure, a privilege...

K: It's always like one side says there's no cause and the other side says there's a cause. I don't need to know that – maybe, maybe not. To be what I am, I don't need to know why things happen or not, and the rest is fiction anyway. So, maybe there is and maybe not. But does it make me more or less as I am? That's the main thing... that's the basis of everything. Does that What I Am gets more if it knows why did this happen? If God is attracted or not? It's all fiction! You make one concept and I make an anti-concept infinitely... there's no end to that. The intellect is an infinite grave of dead concepts.

Q: What you're doing is trimming the intellect and trimming the I, perhaps this helps to be what we cannot *not* be. I know you wouldn't like when I say that... [Laughter]

K: I show the intellect that it is useless. And then the intellect can relax in itself.

Q: I don't think your intellect is useless...

K: You think this intellect is sharp so that your intellect can be sharpened on it?

Q: Yes...

K: That's the Buddhist technique. But again, this is an exercise of failing. What else are we doing here?

Q: There are degrees of failures and kinds of failures...

K: Maybe I lead you to all kinds of failures. [Laughter] It's like the ultimate medicine of Nisargadatta, showing all the ways and failing. Then in the end you even fail to fail because you cannot *not* be. You cannot know yourself as That. The Absolute failing is actually being That what you are: it's the total absolute success. As I said a few days ago, I don't have any keyword, it could be anything that opens the door which is already open... you never know. Why should I talk otherwise? I just talk, talk, talk – just in case.

Q: In Mahabharata towards the end Krishna suffered from Gandhari's curse. Why did Krishna, even after being the Absolute person, not change the script?

K: When Arjuna asked Krishna why do I have to war and kill my friends. If you are the Lord why can't you just change this thing? Krishna said the blueprint is already done by me. I created everything before I even woke up.

Q: And creating another one would be no better?

K: You have to do what you have to do, that's the meaning of it. What is meant to happen will happen because it has already happened.

Q: You mentioned that the next moment after enlightenment you continue taking the cup of coffee...

K: The pointer is that the next sip of coffee is that what is meant to happen. And that what comes after the next sip of coffee is what is meant to happen.

Q: There's no better...

K: There's no more or less in it, it's just the next... Then and then and then and then.

Q: But it is as it is also for us...

K: Yes. Every word is already spoken, every question is already asked, and nothing ever happened. This is silence in action.

Q: So, it's very boring...

K: No, it's just silence in action. It's Life living as Silence.

Q: If there's no 'me', no story, then what is the advantage of it?

K: They asked Ramana why do you speak if you see there's nothing to gain here? Ramana said, if you ask me, it's just sport. It's not because there's a need for it. What else to do?

Q: So, why didn't Krishna change anything?

K: He said even if I would like to change, I could not. He pointed to the helplessness of his Nature. Even the Absolute Creator cannot change his creation because even before Parabrahman started to dream himself as Brahman, the whole dream is dreamt, the whole manifestation is finished.

Q: He *is* the dream...

K: He wakes up and the dream wakes up. His dream is already as absolute and complete as he is. There's no way of changing anything. And the meaning is that there's no control because there are no two. That's the non-duality pointer. Because there are no two, there's no way of controlling yourself. There are no two selves.

Q: Changing is controlling...

K: When you *are* energy, you cannot control energy. Only when you are in an imaginary idea that you *have* energy, than you imagine you can do something. But when you are energy, you are life, there's no way of controlling it.

Q: This is true in all levels of creation...

K: Everyone is that. You can see he cannot be different because he is already as he's meant to be. There's no blaming anyone.

Q: Humans are the only ones who think it could be different...

K: It's wishfool thinking. It's a fool wishing something. It's like an energy-less phantom imagining that he can do something.

Q: The only thing is that the basis of the phantom is real...

K: You can say that the real is experiencing itself as unreal, but the real doesn't become unreal by the unreal experience, that's all. I don't deny the unreal experience. I deny that the unreal experience makes you unreal.

Q: The problem is that we don't realize how this unreal experience...

K: The unreal experience is the dream. That's why it's called a dream, it's unreal.

Q: But the nature of the being is very mysterious...

K: There's no mystery in it. You *are*, there's no mystery! You make it a mystery because the phantom can only remain in a mystery. In knowledge a phantom cannot survive. So the phantom creates a mystery for himself.

Q: But that's also natural...

K: Yes. It's the natural tendency of the phantom. What else can it do? It needs a legacy.

Q: It's like God has a very funny sense of humour...

K: Maybe he has a sixth (sick) sense of humour.

Q: Like Germans...

K: Maybe you have to be German to understand God. [Laughter] You are That and that's all, whether there is humour or not. It's all funny anyway. The biggest joke is that you believe that you exist. No humour will ever be big enough for that joke.

Q: That's His joke too...

K: Yeah, but that's a joke! Trying to see it as a joke is still trying to control it, it's amazing! Trying to understand the joke, it never works. You fail. The joke will always be too big for you to laugh it away. But for what you are, there's no need for humour. That's why peace is incomparable... that's a peace of humour.

Q: That's a sick sense of humour and not the sixth sense of humour...

K: But I don't want to offend the Sikhs, I like the Sikhs.

I always repeat it, enjoy the helplessness. Enjoy the laziness of your nature. You don't have to bear anything.

Q: Laziness means giving up your personal story?

K: The laziest would be that you *are* the cross but you don't have to bear one. But by trying to bear the cross, you suffer. Then there's the passion of Christ. No! *Be* the cross, but don't *have* one!

Q: You mean like sitting in a train and just keeping the luggage on it and not trying to carry it...

K: Yeah. But you try to be the locomotive and the train, Mama mia. Some then say that I'd rather be the train station. [Laughter] The train station is like awareness, the unmovable. Many trains come in and go out, you just witness the train coming in and going out but you are stationary.

Q: There's no need to move there...

K: But even that is a dream! That's where everyone lands, in being the train station. Being the unmovable and not being moved by whatever is moving. That makes you like, 'I am solid and that is not. I am real and that is not'. That's the last and the final delusion.

Q: But the train and the train station always come together...

K: There's only a train because there's a train station. [Laughter]

Q: And there's a train station because there's a train...

K: And there are passengers. They're the worst. [Laughter] The French passengers are unbearable, I tell you. They complain at every station.

You can make a picture that being a train station is more peaceful. That's the idea of peace, being stationary or being silent. By that you make silence an object, you make silence an idea which is different from something else. But for me silence is the train station, the train, the passengers, the moving, the not moving – whatever is, is Silence. Nisargadatta called this as the Absolute block of manifestation, that which is immovable, as every moment is infinite in nature, never created. And in coming nothing comes and in going nothing goes. There's an imaginary time in coming and going, but in coming nothing comes and in going nothing goes.

That's Silence and not the silence of a train station which is always mistaken by many. It's not a silence you can place somewhere. It's not like your nature is more of that and less of this. The natural state is having no natural state, not knowing what is natural and not natural, that's silence. But not 'having' a natural state, and I found my true nature and my true nature is prior to something else. All that prior and beyond and all of that is all fiction. It's just finding a better landing place where I'm not disturbed. But who needs not to be disturbed?

Q [Another visitor]: [Laughing] That's 'me' and don't disturb me, leave me where I am...

K: Leave me there where I'm not, that's the idea. Because you have this idea 'When I'm not, I'm better off. Without me, I'm better off'.

Q: And we make all these competitions, me, me, me...

K: Yeah... 'My realization is deeper than your realization'... even the realized ones competing. There's an enlightenment competition, everywhere... 'My enlightenment is real'.

Q: Yes and I'm more older in the teaching...

K: In the itching? [Laughter] I'm Agent Orange. The French are the world champions in this competition. Even between the French there's a competition – 'I'm more French than you. My ancestors don't come from Russia. I'm from Marie Antoinette. But she was Austrian – Oh shit!' [Laughter]

Q [Another visitor]: So the only thing that keeps the seeker alive is that it thinks that in its absence there's enlightenment?

K: You can say that. The me thinks that me can be better off without the me. You're looking for comfort, and comfort would be where you are not. The end of suffering for you would be the end of the sufferer. You want to go beyond the ego, beyond the sufferer. Then you imagine that without the ego, without the sufferer I would be happy or comfortable. You think that now the ego disturbs you and when there's absence, I'm not disturbed anymore. So, you're looking for peace. Fighting for peace, that keeps the ego alive. You're a peace fighter. That's why I always say 'peace off'.

Q: Also, there's no way out of it?

K: No, in that way you realize yourself. That's the way of consciousness trying to get rid of consciousness because consciousness already is too much. God wants to get rid of God because when God knows God, there are two Gods too many. That's discomfort. When God knows God, he's in the discomfort zone. He's depending on existence, he's doubtful – instantly. This is the first 'I', God knowing himself. You can make it positive by saying that God wants to know himself out of loving caring about himself. No! He's just pissed that he has to exist. So pissed off! Then he wants to go back to where he belongs, but the more he wants to go back, the more he confirms the one who wants to go back. That's the trick you cannot get out of.

This is waking up... that you wake up from the idea that there's any place better than this, and in that you cannot exist as a relative me, that's all. You can only exist as a relative me when the grass there is better than here. When the absence of the 'me' is better than the presence of the 'me'. That keeps the 'me' alive. One idea needs another idea. The idea, the concept that the absence is better than the presence keeps that suffering thing alive.

Q [Another visitor]: Will God always be jealous of Itself?

K: When God exists God is jealous about the God that doesn't need to exist. It's a crazy thing, the moment God exists he's even jealous about himself. How big can this joke be?

Q [Another visitor]: Who is it who makes this joke?

K: You! An accident happened. God out of this Absolute not knowing himself woke up to know himself. There's no one who made it.

Q: For the mind...

K: There's no 'for the mind'.... There's no guilt in anything, there's no sin. It just happened, that's why it's called as an accident. What is an accident? Is it something that you want?

Q: No no...

K: You see... it's an accident. You still want to find the guilty one and if you find him, you want to kill him. That's the hate for himself. You hate yourself so much that you want to kill yourself. Not out of love you want to know yourself. You fake it as love because maybe the one you want to kill shows up.

Q [Another visitor]: Yesterday you mentioned to meditate on the one who's seeing...

K: No. Give attention only to that Seer you cannot see.

Q: Yeah...

K: Where's the yeah in it? [Laughter]

Q [Another visitor]: Now you say even consciousness is too much...

K: Yes because consciousness is something you can experience. You have to experience to be conscious but what you are doesn't need to be conscious to be what it is. That consciousness you can experience you cannot be.

Q: We need to be still...

K: There's no 'still'... there's no 'we' in it, say 'I'!

Q: Do I have to be aware of the one who's looking?

K: If you would've listened to me, you wouldn't have had this question. I tell you give attention to that what you cannot see.

Q: Then it stops...

K: When did it start? You already have to be someone that sees. You already have to be the 'I' which can be an experience, it needs to be experienced. And out of the first 'I' experience, all the rest arises. But if you are That what is part of that what you cannot see, that is the Absolute Seer which can never be seen. Give all attention to that what you can never see but you cannot *be* that what you can never see. That what you can see is what? Beginning of false. That is the meditation – if you ask me. But people wouldn't call it a meditation.

Just give attention by being That what can never be seen in any way. This is just the tradition of Ramana... Be the Absolute Seer which can never be seen in any scenery or non-scenery.

Q: You cannot say it starts?

K: There is no start in it. This is a direct killing of that what you are not. Just by being what you are you kill everything what you are not – that's all. Only by being what you are, by being what you cannot *not* be, that which can never be experienced. And by being that, there's nothing else to do, or not to do.

Q: But so many say...

K: Forget the many, listen to me.

Q: It cannot be understood...

K: It doesn't *need* to be understood! You don't have to understand, you don't have to know, you don't have to experience that what you are to be that what you are. Just be That what doesn't need to be anything and that is satisfaction. Be that Peace which doesn't need peace... mind will never stop fighting for peace. Consciousness will always fight for peace but it cannot find it anyway. So let consciousness play the game and fight for peace. But all this fighting for peace creates war.

As I just said, the peace that you can find is not worth having. The peace you are, you never lost. For that, you don't have to fight and that's the end of war. But any moment you fight for peace, you are a warrior.

Q: So, to give up this...

K: Don't give up anything. Just give up giving up. Surrender the surrendering! There is nothing for you to surrender to be. Surrender the surrendering, devote the devotion by being what you are. Kill all ideas just by being what you are, there's no other way. That's Buddha saying there's only one way out of suffering but not by ending suffering. By being in spite of the sufferer, in spite of whatever. And not because you end suffering. Not because you found peace or you found knowledge. Just by being in spite and not because.

Q: I thought I understood it by seeing that you are not part of the movie. But you go beyond...

K: No I don't go beyond. I just talk to that what you are. It's now or never. It's not something you will become by imagining something, like a divine mystical marriage and all the dances and things. No, the question is what is *this*? This you can call as Light, or Self realizing itself. What to do?

Q [Another visitor]: You say the end of the suffering is being in spite of the suffering...

K: To be that what is in spite of whatever you can imagine.

Q: But is it possible to say...

K: It's not possible. This is just what it is. And not that it is possible when you enter *nirvana* bullshit. By just being in spite of whatever, the unenlightened one drops. It doesn't create an enlightened one. There's no enlightenment experience because that what you are doesn't need any enlightenment experience to be what it is. And that what needs an enlightenment experience to be what it is, is a phantom – that's all. So be in spite. All the ideas that you are unenlightened drop at the moment when you are what you are. And by that there's no need for any enlightenment... and *that* you can call enlightenment!

Q: Is it possible to say...

K: It's not possible. [Laughter] You can say whatever, it's even possible, but it's not possible. You want to put it in a phrase which can stay.

Q: You said everything is grace in action...

K: I can say silence in the dream of movement. The dream of movement means that in coming something comes and in going something goes, that's the dream. Otherwise there's no dream. It's your idea that in coming something comes and in going something goes, *that* is the dream which makes you a phantom.

Q: When there's suffering...

K: There's no '*when* there's suffering!' *Now* there's suffering, look at it! Look at these people! [Laughter]

Q: Now there's no suffering...

K: There's always suffering, there's always discomfort: the

experience of discomfort never started and it will never end. You can only realize yourself in discomfort – the discomfort of separation – otherwise you cannot realize yourself. You can only realize yourself in the Trinity which is that the father is different from the spirit and the son. That's the way you realize yourself, so there's always discomfort.

But the comfort of the Heart, the kingdom of the Heart cannot be entered in that Trinity. So, they are not *different* from discomfort but the comfort is realizing itself in discomfort. The ease is realizing itself in a disease. This is a disease, but you cannot get rid of the disease because you are the ease which is realizing itself in a disease. And you cannot get out of it. But by all the experiences of illness and disease, you don't get sick. You are always That what cannot get sick by itself.

Experiencing yourself in a relative experience of a 'me', doesn't make you a 'me' or any experiencer. But you cannot avoid it. You experience yourself as stupid, and you are anyway... you must be stupid to realize yourself in spite of whatever. But you have to. But by all the ignorance you can experience you don't become ignorant. The Knowledge you are is uninterrupted. The Knowledge that you are cannot be changed by anything, come on!

Q: When Buddha was talking about the end of suffering, what is it exactly that he meant?

K: He said that the suffering ended because he saw that it will never end. Can you grasp that? [Laughter] The end of 'you' is that you see that you will never end because in that there's no 'me'.

Q: I want to understand...

K: Because you want to understand, you are stupid.

Q: I know. That's why I'm trying to be precise...

K: By trying to be precise, you really lose. Don't try anything.

Q: Just by accepting the fact that suffering will never end...

K: No. It's not an acceptance because you will never accept that.

Q: Accepting the non-acceptance of the fact...

K: Even that is not good enough. It's not depending on 'you' – come on! You want to make existence depending on your bloody acceptance? It's not about you baby. He wants to survive. He is like the Lama from Denmark who wants to survive in the infinite as a cubic centimeter of consciousness. I still want to be there where the Infinite is. I want to be the finite in the infinite, especially 'me'. It's amazing! I want to remain in Knowledge as a knower. You will not remain there. In Knowledge there's no knower – only in ignorance there's a knower.

Q [Another visitor]: Are you sure you read Ole Nydahl right?

K: Yes. I met him in Australia in 1993 in Perth. What an asshole. Look at my beloved family, look at my nice wife, showing off like hell and sitting there like a Buddha and telling everyone what they have to do. Fuck you! Who are you?

Q: He had a very nice wife...

K: Yes. That's why I hate him. [Laughter] Then showing off his bloody holy family as if everyone should know that my life is perfect, my harmony.

Q: She died...

K: Everyone dies sooner or later. Big news! She was already dead when I saw her because she was only the wife of Ole Nydahl. These people who show off with flowers and things – my happy wife, my happy girl friend. All this fake look can be done. Fuck you all! I love you all? No. I hate you anyway. [Groaning] [Laughter]

This tendency that I have to destroy everything I cannot stop. And I love it. It's like a child on the beach that makes castles and when time comes to leave he just breaks it – Fuck it all, I go home and sleep. [Laughter]

Q: Are you really mad at him or you just don't care?

K: I love to be mad. Wow, what an energy – anger. [Groaning] [Laughter] Anger for one second and then the next moment you blow it up. It doesn't stick on me, come on. But the moment you don't want to be angry, the anger sticks on you. That's the whole technique. The moment you want to love everybody, you hate him anyway. And you know already that you cannot do it, but you try. Then you try to live, you try to exist, you try to do whatever. Trying is not enough, just be that: don't try to be that and make it a concept of how it has to be. Happy families for sure is not that what you need! [Laughter] Maybe you have one but you don't have to show off to everybody... 'Look how perfect my family is or look how perfect I am. I'm a master and if you follow me you can be as perfect as me'. That's like a prostitute who says that I can satisfy you. Be my customer, give your attention because maybe I can make you happy. [Groaning] No one gets anything here and that's enough.

Q [Another visitor]: Is Silence same as Absolute?

K: No. It's two different names. [Laughter]

Q [Another visitor]: What was the question?

K: I don't know but I answered. I don't have to know the question to make an answer. [Laughter]

The Absolute doesn't need silence and the silence doesn't need the Absolute – finished! It doesn't have to be same same. Do you want to fix it again? I know you want to control it by knowing that Absolute is same as silence and maybe silence is peace. Then you put everything in one basket [Laughter] I know the Absolute is a bit this one, a bit that one, a bit love, a bit laughter, a bit peace. [Laughter] The witch again collecting the ingredients of 'my' life – wanting to know this and wanting to know that.

If I say just be in *spite* of whatever – who needs to know if it's silence or whatever? It's all fucking names for no-one-knows-what.

Q [Another visitor]: I always use this 'Who Am I' question as a tranquilizer...

K: Yeah. Then you abuse it.

Q: What is the authentic way to redirect the attention to what I Am?

K: Meditation for inner peace, meditation for better life, meditation for whatever is work for me... it's not meditation. The nature of meditation is action without intention.

Q: How to take the intention away?

K: You will fail. It will happen when it happens but not because you want it. There's no 'how' in it. When it's meant to happen there will be meditation without a meditator. But until then there's a meditator trying to get something out of his non-action. That's the way it is. You wish for wishlessness but it doesn't work. You have a desire of not having a desire and you meditate for that. It's an infinite way, like a dog trying to bite his own tail. It's like trying to get something out of something. But in that what I point to, there's no getting. It has absolutely no consequence. You are for sure not interested in giving attention to the Absolute who has no consequence to this so-called dream or life. Your interest is that you want to have a better life, better comfort. You want to have enlightenment because for you it means that you will be ever happy. All the problems will be gone and existence will totally take care. These are your ideas about enlightenment or awakening. That's your interest.

Q: So the interest has to go in its own time...

K: The interest only has to go to that what is satisfaction but without any consequences.

Q: And without any intention?

K: No. You have to make *absolute* intention to be That what is in spite of any intention. It's a paradox. You have to make a *koan* that cannot be broken. That what is not in any future event or in any past event and is not even there now. Giving only attention to that what is not even in the now. That is only by being what is in spite and not trying to put it in some frame. So, even 'now' is too late. What to do?

But maybe you have to fail more into the relative world until you're really fed up from the relative thing. Who knows? Everything is possible. But maybe that will take a long long time to burn out your desires or *vasanas*. Maybe it never ends or maybe it ends the next moment. You'll never know. It's so unpredictable. You're not even sure if there was a past or will there be a future. And who is alive now and what will come out of it? All of this is fiction. What is there?

I can only talk to the carelessness that is there, which never cares about anything. That's all I can do. Just the flavor of carelessness, the taste of tastelessness, being in spite of all your imaginary needs and things which can never be fulfilled. And what you are never needs any fullfillment because it is satisfaction itself. Pointing and talking to that what has no need of any change. That's what Ramana calls the highest *tapas* that you can do – listening to that what you are from that what you are – I to I. This good company you cannot create. So, what to do?

And if this fire of Heart is there, it will burn down the house anyway but not because you want to burn down the house. So, when you are the fire there's no way that someone can remain in that fire of life. Now whatever you try is to put it down. The crazy wisdom is fire without any direction. This directionlessness of existence you cannot stir up, it's already here. It's unpredictable – whatever it is. Anything is possible, everything is possible, any moment. But it's impossible not to be. So why postpone it?

And that will not come by meditation. Again I have to say that you can meditate forever and you will not attain what you are. You are here now in spite of it and not when you give intention to That alone what is in spite... it's all too late in that sense. Be that what is in-no-sense anyway. And that what you are will never be sensed by what you are. Be That what is in no sense (innocence) and in all the senses, that what it is. You're neither in sense or in no sense what you are. Even the idea of innocence is one too many.

That certainty that you are, no one can give you. That Absolute certainty, which is always absolutely present. This – which is doubtlessness in its nature – cannot be produced by anything. It was never lost and it cannot be gained back. In that sense, I cannot give you anything. You already *are* That what cannot be given or taken away by anyone. And the rest is fiction anyway.

Q: So we need to be reminded again and again and again?

K: That what needs to be reminded is not what you are. That what you are doesn't need to be reminded.

Q: Then why are we coming and listening to that?

K: Do you think you're really coming? I doubt that you are even here. Who came? And who will go? There's no 'why' you're coming. You're not coming for anything! There's an experience of coming and an experience of going but in coming no one comes and in going no one goes. There's no 'why' in it. You just want to make a reason out of it. But you don't need one.

Q: I wonder...

K: I always wonder after whatever I say, these questions still come.

Q: Finish...

K: There's no finish. You're French you're not Finnish. [Laughter]

Q: I want to be finished...

K: She wants to go to Hell-sinki. [Laughter] If you can survive in Helsinki, you will make it. It's the most boring place. Everyone is drunk and stinking and vomiting and the suicide rate is the highest in the world in Helsinki.

Q: I tried many extremes...

K: Try suicide. Then at least we don't have to listen to you. If you don't like to listen to yourself, why should we? [Laughter] If she doesn't even like herself, why should we like her? Relieve us.

Q: I just wanted to be reminded...

K: Be reminded that I don't need you.

Q: [Laughing] But I need you and this is the point. That's the problem actually...

K: Not mine.

Q: It's mine.

K: But she wants to make it my problem too that she has a problem. That's actually everyone who meets someone, they want to make their problem the other's problem. How are you? How do you do?... but don't tell me. Already what I have is enough. I already have too much, I don't need more.

Anyone else who wants to be winded or re-winded? Whining about whatever...

Q [Another visitor]: What is art and does it express anything that's worth being expressed?

K: *This* is art. This is art without an artist.

Q: And the art *with* an artist?

K: ...is shit. Every musician tells you that, every painter tells you that. Painting happens when I'm not there, music happens when I'm not there, when the muse is playing but not me. I can only amuse myself when I'm not. That's is a-musing, when the musician is not playing the music anymore and the music is, when art is, when Self is, and not when someone's there who makes nice music. Then it's nice music but not art.

Q [Another visitor]: Is it wrong...

K: Yes. [Laughter] If you start a question that way it's wrong already.

Q: I really feel romantic with myself...

K: That's very rare, normally she hates herself deeply. Right now she gets romantic because she has a hangover. [Laughter]

Q: I feel really romantic feeling Ramana, Nisargadatta and you around...

Q [Another visitor]: I can imagine! [Laughter]

K: To me it really sounds like a nightmare. Being surrounded by me, that would really be a nightmare and with Nisargadatta on top of it! And then Happy-Nappy – what a party! [Laughter] It doesn't sound so romantic I think.

Q [Another visitor]: What are we trying to escape from?

K: From yourself. You are too much for yourself. Your imaginary self is too much for yourself so you try to escape yourself and you will never succeed. That's called 'seeking' – trying to escape yourself, trying to find another dimension, another whatever, better place, better understanding, better whatever. Trying to escape yourself.

Q: The seeking sucks...

K: The seeker sucks. The succeeding sucks, that's why it's called suck-seeding. The sucker sucks, always looking for a big satisfaction in this Milky Way. You try to escape and by that you are always not here. You are always somewhere in an imagined past or future, even 'now' you make as an imagination. Then you want to escape in the now: that's the Tolle escape technique.

Q [Another visitor]: UG had some extraordinary things happening with his body...

K: He was lying the moment he opened his mouth and everyone believed him. He said that an enlightened one's underwear doesn't smell. Then the ladies who made the laundry went and really smelled and they were quite surprised. [Laughter] I like him because he was lying about anything. He was just barking and everyone was like yes, yes, yes... they really believed what he said. He was the biggest liar ever. There was not one true word coming from his mouth and he said it himself. But everyone still thought there must be something. Everyone was still esoteric and was looking after some miracle bullshit and that it has to be special. And he was just serving that idea that someone was there who was special. [Pointing to a visitor] She is still in that imaginary feeling that UG was a special guy in spite of him saying that I'm just a barking dog and don't believe any word I say. In his first book he mentioned about the whole calamity that happened with his body, all bullshit. [Groaning] [Laughter]

Q: I'm heading for a collapsing...

K: You still think you can collapse?

Q: It's like an implosion...

K: We all hope for that. [Laughter] You may implode now. You're not alone in wishing that. [Pointing to another visitor] You too actually. There are many here, just implode now. Explosion is too much mess. [Laughter] It has to be a clean bye bye. But everyone wants to explode and make a mess all over the universe. Then I'm everything. No, you have to implode.

Q: I'll give it a shot...

K: And tell us how it was. But first implode and then give us a report of the journey. [Laughter]

Q [Another visitor]: Do you think UG Krishnamurti's calamity was a stroke?

K: You can fish, I have no idea. Maybe a brain stroke. They say enlightenment is a sickness, like a body disease. It's all about the body anyway. If this tool is not there, there's no experience. No idea.

It's all part of the consciousness: all the side effects and things and all the consequences are all part of this dream. In What you are, there's no such thing, but everyone waits for side effects. As I said in the beginning, you have to meditate on that one which has no side effects and no consequence. But any enlightenment, any experience of a side effect, any consequence is not it. It's *by* the way not *because* of the way.

Q [Another visitor]: Yesterday you said that a teacher who rejects you or asks you to go away and says that I'm not a guru, is a guru anyway...

K: Yes. The one who doesn't want to be a guru is already a guru. No way out.

Q: So what about you?

K: I am but I am not. I cannot avoid it. Actually you can take me as whatever you like. If I say I am or I am not, I am neither. That's what I like about being what I am, I don't have to define it in any way, or not define it. I can define myself or not define myself, it makes no difference if I'm a teacher or not a teacher. It's okay anyway, who gives a shit? If none of that makes me more or less as I am, I can be a teacher, why not? Or underwear or whatever. I can even be German – worst case scenario – or a Jew. Two chosen ones meeting. [Laughter]

When you are already That, you don't know what you are and what you are not. So, you are even an underwear, you are a teacher. Why reject anything? Or why not?

Q: It looks like you are just being a mirror...

K: When I listen to you I become French I tell you. [Laughter]

Q: You said that you can be whatever you are or not. So it's like whatever comes to the mirror it reflects...

K: But I'm not the mirror because then I'm mirroring something else. Your esoteric things don't work here. [Laughter] But it sounds good that I'm mirroring something. I don't resonate with anything I tell you.

Q [Another visitor]: I have a friend who was abandoned by her Indian parents and was adopted by Western parents and raised there. What would you say about that?

K: I don't know. She should kill her parents in the West and come back to India. [Laughter] Where does she live?

Q: She's an Indian living in Switzerland...

K: That's worse. Who wants to be in a place where they level the grass with scissors? But it's the same with Australians. If you're an Australian it's like an Indian living in Switzerland. They have such identity crisis... like they are in Aboriginal land and they don't belong there. They're around like balloons levitating around the country. They have no ground.

Everyone has an identity crisis, that's nothing special. Everyone feels abandoned from Existence. That's nothing fucking special, that's everyone's story. But everyone is in a competition about who is more abandoned. An Indian living in Switzerland is just a life story and she feels very important in it. And everyone is listening and feeling pity and comparing their childhoods. Everyone has a story going on. It's best to ignore it. Then she's fine. If no one would listen to it she would just stop talking about it. But you always find a shrink around her who's listening... 'Yes, I feel with you'. Taking a bath in a pool of pitifulness.

Anyone else has a good story? [Laughter] We can make a competition whose childhood was the worst and who's the most sickest here... it becomes just like a waiting room for a doctor. How many kidneys do you have? You still have one? Ha ha ha! I don't even have a liver anymore.

Q [Another visitor]: I'm a parent...

K: Should I pity you now? [Laughter]

Q: Once I wanted my parents to leave and now it's my children asking me to leave...

K: You're guilty for both. As a child you want to escape your parents because you hate to be controlled. And now you are the controller and someone wants to escape you.

Q: Because I think I'm special?

K: Of course. Every mother thinks she's the most special and her baby is the most special baby. My diamond baby, my indigo baby! [Laughter]

Q: But we only talk about the parent and not the child...

K: Both are fucked if you ask me! When you're the parent it's like being Maria the mother of Jesus and you're fucked. When you're the son you're fucked again. Both have to go. Nisargadatta says you are a child of a barren woman because what you are was never born and will never die. So just be That what you are which never has any parent and never will be a parent of anyone. Apparently you are a parent – that's all. It's only ap*parent*ly but not in reality. It appears like you are, but you are not.

Q: Talking about being a parent...

K: You feel abandoned. Here's another one. [Laughter] I remember my father standing in front of me because I was just with my suitcase on my way to San Francisco. The day before was the last day milking cows with my father. He said you cannot go, my whole life will be over, crying and all this drama. And then I just took my luggage and left. If you really look into it, you cannot do it because the burden was put on you that you are so important for one's life and his reason of being alive depends on you and you still have to go. That was the best I ever did for myself and him. Because then my sister took over the farm.

The only way to be out of all that drama is being 'What you are' which was never anyone's parent or child, and by all those happenings, nothing ever happened anyway. If you try to fix anything in that, being a parent and child of anyone, you will work forever. You will go to her [Pointing to a visitor] forever... she's a family constipation expert. I don't want to destroy her job... in fact I tell her your job will never be over. There will always be someone who feels the drama from his childhood. 'And my uncle touched me and later on someone told me it was not appropriate'. [Laughter] What to do? I have no idea.

I can only give you the ultimate medicine. For the body it's an infinite story of a disease and it always tries to fix something what is unfixable. You only have an identity crisis because you're identified. One leads to the other. The moment you exist, you're identified with existence. Then you have an existential crisis – instantly. The moment God knows God as existence, he's in a crisis of Himself. Then he creates his own family, just to hold on to something. The whole drama of having a family.

When I really look at the news about what happens in families, for sure it's not the best place to be. In Texas there was a family that was raising a child by water boarding... disciplining your child with water boarding! Every day you read something about families, the most dangerous place on earth, for both parents and child. Having relatives is a worst case scenario. *Being* relative is already the worst, then having relatives! [Laughter] Then fighting for your family, always *having* a reason to kill someone for your family. Everyone says I'll shoot anyone for my family. There's always a good reason to release the anger out on someone else. I do this out of love for my family. I'm ruthless in my job and I want to make millions, for my family. Doing all the bad things with the excuse 'for my family'. All the wars are 'for my family'. What to do?

Was there any peace in any family? Can there be a peaceful family? Why do soldiers go to war? Maybe just to get rid of the family or the mother or the wife. Why are men hunters? He's happy to be out. Going fishing, that's the next famous thing.

See you tomorrow for the last nail in the coffin.

20th Feb 2016
Tiruvannamalai

Chapter Six

That What You Are Doesn't Need Any Peace And That What Needs Peace Will Never Find Peace

∽

K: Okay, last day. Do your best! [Laughter]

Q: You said relationship never works...

K: It never works. It comes by itself and it goes by itself... and in between there is... what?

Q: Whatever you make of it...

K: You don't make anything out of anything, I tell you. You make shit when you eat. You're a shit factory, you know that! Ladies are always interested in relationship. It's amazing! Permanent! Working on a relationship.

Q [Another visitor]: You haven't made fun of Canadians yet...

K: There are not so many... why should I care? I talk a lot about Eckhart Tolle.

Q: He is not a Canadian...

K: But you took him as a refugee... so you're now punished by a lot of rain there. You even took John De Ruiter. But then you have so much space you don't see him that much.

Q: I think he got frozen up there...

K: That's why he speaks so slowly [Laughter] One is quite cursed when he has a nationality. Any nationality sucks... you don't have to make a competition who sucks more.

Q [Another visitor]: I dare not speak...

K: Since a few years I tried to shut her up but it's impossible... so I'm totally useless. She proves that I'm a failure. They all prove that I'm failing. Some I know from twenty years and they prove that I fail as a teacher. They've never learnt anything. They still look at me with the same eyes... 'What the fuck is he talking about? I don't know what he says... but okay... I give him another day'. [Laughter]

Q [Another visitor]: I'm not so long with you...

K: You have been there long enough. If you don't get it in five days, you will never get it in a hundred years. Now I have to be like Nisargadatta... if one has been there for ten days, out! If you don't get it now, try another time... come again in ten years. But normally I don't talk in my living room so I can't kick people out so easily.

Q [Another visitor]: So it is about turning your attention only to That?

K: No... It's just *being* attention. That's giving absolute attention to That what you are... by being attention but not *having* attention. Okay?

Q: No...

K: You claim that you have attention or you can give attention, that's the joke. Being attention you have no direction. Attention has no special attention, it is just attention but not giving attention.

Q: So what about giving attention to That?

K: There is no *giving* attention! You cannot give attention. You give attention to That by *being* attention but this is not giving anything. Listen to me! Thank God this is the last talk. [Laughter] She still asks how to do that? Is anyone even listening to me?

Q: How to be?

K: How not to be? [Laughter] Try *not* to be, come on!

Q: I tried but it doesn't work...

K: And by that you have these bloody questions.

Q [Another visitor]: If it's meant to happen that you find yourself ten meters under water and there's no survival anymore, will Consciousness make a unique way for a unique phantom?

K: No! For what? It's happy that it gets rid of you. Unique phantom! [Laughter] She wants to become a Unicorn. No. In that the body goes, the Universe goes, everything goes... because there's no survival possible, because that what *is* Self drops the *idea* of self... and by that there's no 'me', there's no Universe, there's no experience, nothing is possible! So, what to do? Do you want to wait for that? You make a special circumstance again, which may never happen.

Q: It's not in my hands...

K: Whose hand? What is not in your hand? [Laughing]

Q [Another visitor]: When you say be lazy...

K: No... be That what is lazy! In that laziness you don't exist because you're even too lazy to be.

Q: Does that mean less painful choices arise?

K: No. There's laziness... there's no one who even gets up by anything. It's total laziness of That what you are... nothing is arising from there. That which is Silence is laziness. Nothing happens... it's like uninterrupted That what you are. Ramana calls it a flat line... the laziness of being what you are is a flat line. Nothing ever happens! Just be that! Laziness you cannot exercise, you cannot do. It's not about you trying to do laziness or something.

Q: The doingness that arises is not you?

K: You don't even know what you are and what you are not... because you are even too lazy to know what you are. You're even too lazy to be lazy! [A chair breaks] You are like this chair. The nature of laziness is to be too lazy even to be lazy... so it doesn't *need* to be lazy! Anything can happen... but in that, no one is doing anything. There's an absolute non-doership in that laziness. But it doesn't mean nothing happens. You make laziness as a lazy bastard sitting somewhere. No, laziness is the nature of life living... because life living needs no energy. There's no effort in life living. There's an effortlessness of being, that's all. That's laziness... and not me making an effort for something... making an effort to *not* make an effort!

That laziness which is *jñāna* is what you are and this laziness doesn't allow any *jñāna*. There's no *jñāna* in *jñāna* There's no one who has to stay there. That's the beauty of laziness... that no one needs to stay there... and there's no one who *can* stay there. You cannot achieve it, you cannot attain it. It's unattainable... that what you are. That is laziness. So be what you cannot *not* be, that's laziness. But not by understanding it or trying to become it or anything.

Q [Another visitor]: This is equivalent of dropping the doer?

K: No... even the doer doesn't need to be dropped for that. Nothing has to go, nothing has to come for it. You will always be too much anyway...even when you're not, you're too much.

Q: There's no 'I' thought...

K: Even no 'I' thought is one 'I' thought too many... because then you make it dependent again... on no 'I' thought. It's absolutely independent of presence or absence!

Q: It is an effortless state of being...

K: It is an effortlessness of being... effort or no-effort is still too much effort. The effortlessness is laziness. There's neither effort nor no effort... that's *neti-neti* of all of that.

Q: Is it possible for something to happen in that state that Consciousness is not aware of?

K: Consciousness can be aware or not... who gives a shit?

Q: I can sit doing nothing with no 'I' thought, okay...

K: We're talking about That what you are in nature and not how you can achieve it.

Q: I'm not talking about achieving...

K: But you want to make it something.

Q: If I'm taking shit, there needs to be some 'I' that thinks about how do I make my way to the bathroom [Laughter]. I'm just saying... make sense, say something! What you are saying is a total *koan*...

K: That's what I am... a total *koan*! I'm not here to make sense for anyone. I'm not here to give anyone a tool of achieving something. I really have no interest of anyone understanding anything here... you know that!

Q: I know that. But still... [Laughter] I offer my head on the plate you know...

K: That is one head too many. [Laughter] Who is interested in your head?

Q: I'm interested...

K: But no one else, I tell you! I have no interest in your head... and you can be the head master of the whole Universe, I still have no interest. You can be the *avatar* of all time... you can know everything... you can control everything... and I have no interest in it because it still *depends* on something. There's still a little whatever who wants to be big. And even the *avatar* who controls the whole cosmos, is still... what? Helpless! He is controlled by his control. What are you looking for? For peace or for control? That's the main question! You want to control yourself? Or you want to be that what is peace, which is satisfaction... What is your interest? Controlling everything by your ideas, by intellect or you want to have peace with yourself? What is your interest?

Q: You know that...

K: But whatever I hear from you is trying to control and not peace. Only a *koan* can bring you peace because it breaks the 'me'. It breaks your idea that you can control something. This giving up cannot be done by you. This surrendering to That what you are cannot be done by you trying to surrender. This surrendering is being what you are... but only That what you are can be that... and not one who tries to be that. In that sense, I jump around... and you try to catch me. Catch me if you can!

Q: I'm trying... [Laughter]

K: I know everyone tries to put me in a corner and say, 'Come on! Make sense'. For me there's no corner that can hold me. I cannot be cornered by anything. But everyone tries to corner me, I know that. Putting me somewhere and thinking... 'Oh there he is. Now I know where he talks from, this is his reference point, this is where he's teaching from, this is his teaching, this is what he's saying'. No! I don't give you anything! The moment you think you've cornered me, I'm already gone!

Q: I'm not trying to put you in a corner or label you...

K: But you just asked me to make sense... and I tell you if I would try to make sense, I would be cornered again... by an idea that I have to make sense. Then I'd corner myself.

Q: But that's your problem... [Laughter]

K: And then I'd make your problem as my problem. But I'm not here to make your problem as my problem.

Q: We need to share something for some kind of communication...

K: No we don't have to share anything, that's the problem. There's no sharing here. There's no big piece of cake we have to share. The piece of cake you can share... but not peace. There's no 'share' in peace. You become a stock holder of peace... 'This is my share of peace'. There's no 'my' peace in Peace... there's no ownership.

Q: In a sense we are all That...

K: There's no sense in it, there's no 'we' in it... you have to be fucking alone in it! There's no 'me', there's no 'we'... the 'whole Universe' is not there in it... especially not 'we'!

Q [Another visitor]: Then?

K: Fuck off! [Laughter] This is the last talk, I need to be...

Q [Another visitor]: If I'm on the other side of the divide I'd not be fair to myself...

K: You don't have to be fair to yourself... and no one will ever be fair to yourself. Who needs fairness?

Q: It depends upon...

K: *What* depends upon? That who needs fairness is a phantom who tries to get attention...

Q: That's all Advaita...

K: I'm not here to pamper a bloody phantom. I'm not a pamperer. I'm here to kill... for sure, if I can! But not by pampering you...

Q: Why is it not working Karl?

K: Maybe your control system is still running too high, if you ask me. What can I do if you're still interested in control? Who am I? That's what Ramana said, you have to be dry when you come to me. Dry so that you can make the fire burn and not being one who is interested in trying to control the fire.

Q: It's not up to me. What can I do?

K: You are not finished with your intellectual understanding... you still try to control something here. It doesn't work and for sure it's not pleasant. But I cannot help you in that. You have to try as much as you can. I cannot burn you out... you have to burn out yourself. When that happens, I'm there for you but not before. Otherwise I'd fight with you... but why should I fight with you? For what?

And I don't have to be right to be right... because I'm anyway right. [Laughter] Whatever I say there's a doubtlessness... I am That what is right anyway. Even if it's the biggest bullshit I say, I'm right. [Laughter] This comes from the doubtlessness of the certainty of what I am. But everything else is what? Fighting for some bullshit! I don't have to fight for what I am. I agree with UG Krishnamurthi... I'm a free man because I'm not in contradiction with anything. I'm not in any conflict with whatever you can imagine. There's no conflict for me... as I have nothing to defend. I have no reference point of some wisdom or something that I have to defend. I can be the biggest asshole on earth and I'm still what I am.

Q: If your tongue were a little longer and words were a little rounder... [Laughter]

K: [Laughing] No. Round me up baby.

This is laziness... that the whole universe cannot give me anything. Who needs that some people agree to what I say? I couldn't care less.

Q: There's a consensus of thought...

K: We are here for fun and not for consents... that what you are doesn't need any consent. Who needs to be harmonized here? With what? I like this disharmony.

Q: Being itself...

K: But being Itself doesn't need any harmony... it *is* harmony. And that what needs harmony is an artificial one. You fish for an artificial harmony by trying to make sense out of things because then you're comfortable, because then you land in a consent.

Q: A relative being trying to align itself with the Absolute being... what's the problem in that?

K: But who is interested in being in harmony with the Universe? I have no interest. Don't ask me! Go to a teacher who can give you some peace.

Q: Why do you speak to someone who is not that interested in you? Why speak to the relative phantoms?

K: I don't speak to phantoms. You think I speak to phantoms here? I don't talk to you... if I would see you, I would not talk to you. Why should I go to that intellectual fight? For what? I'm only interested in that what I am... that which is behind you, that what is not just talking now or trying to survive. I'm not interested in the survivor. For me you don't even exist. Why should I fight with someone who doesn't even exist? What is in it for me if I win a fight with someone who doesn't even exist?

Q: It's not a fight...

K: It's a fight! You fight for peace... that's a permanent fighting.

Q: It's inquiry...

K: It's not an inquiry... this is fighting for peace, just be honest! You want to have a peace of mind and for that you fight. It's futile. Your mind will never be peaceful. And who is interested in a peace of mind? Only the mind is interested in a peace of mind, and for that it fights... because if there really would be peace, there would be no mind! So it better fight for peace!

Survival system – that's all. Survival system of a phantom 'me' who actually knows by intuition that in peace it cannot exist anymore. It tries very hard to be in the quicksand of lies... but sooner or later the quicksand sucks you in anyway.

Q: To where?

K: To where no one can be.

Q: Yes, that's the idea... [Laughter]

K: I'm the quicksand for you, but you still resist. I'm too quick for you that's why it's called a 'quick' sand.

Q: Please be a bit slower so that I can get sucked in... [Laughter]

K: [Laughing] No... you want to make me a bit slower so that you can find some anchor in that quicksand... 'I want some anchor where I can anchor my ship. I need some ground, please give me some ground?' No. I don't give you any ground. I'm grinding you, like a milling... milling of the 'me', then you become Mr. Miller. And then the tendency of milling just continues, because you would be Mr. Miller who's milling Mr. Miller.

Q: You should give it a chance Karl...

K: No, no, no. [Laughter] I like when they say 'on the day of execution'... for me it's always execution. I like execution. Execution is being what you are... executing the false just by being what you are. That's execution... moment by moment... and not in any future time.

Q: Right now it's happening...

K: No it's not happening.

Q: Why not?

K: It's not a 'happening'.

Q: Who says?

K: I say...

Q: Who's you?

K: I am the Absolute talking to the Absolute.

Q: What gives you the right to say something like that? What is there is also here...

K: It's not there and it's not here!

Q: Then who's talking?

K: That's the question... Who's talking here? And who's listening? Tell me!

Q: That's for you to say...

K: [Laughing] Now he slips out... see you learnt something! [Laughter] Finally he becomes as slippery as me. You're absolutely slippery, you slip out of everything.

Q: I'm hoping you'll make a mistake... [Laughter] I'm talking here for all of you. [Laughter] [Clapping] Sorry, I keep quiet now...

K: [Referring to the visitor] I'm here to be killed for everyone.

Q: Excuse me, that was a mistake...

K: You are here for yourself not for anyone else. I like execution... every moment you are the executioner, the execution and that what is executed. This is your execution, right now! This is Attention giving attention to Itself. This is an execution day... execution, execution, execution! There's no moment without execution... and nothing has to be executed in it, I like that. Where does it come from? They talk about the execution day. No! *This* is execution... this and this and this and this!

Being the executioner, the execution and that what is being executed... the killer, the killing, and the killed you are. And you are killing time which is not there. You try to kill the time which is not there! You try to get rid of the separation which is never there, never was. You have to execute the executioner by being That what never can be executed... that makes you very cute. [Laughter] The cutest of the cute because you are that what can never be executed. This is just a word game now, but go into it... just sink into that. You are the way you pronounce yourself... and from where you pronounce yourself... and from where you realize yourself. That makes you!

Q [Another visitor]: This non-stop burning and pain which happens is also part of the survival system?

K: No, that's already execution... everything is execution! Any moment you experience yourself, you want to kill yourself. Every moment, you are that who wants to execute everything because you're fed up with it. You don't want to be a relative God. You don't want to be a relative person. You don't want to be in any way relative... so you want to execute yourself. You want to shoot yourself. You seek a way out of this... whatever this is. There was never any moment when Consciousness didn't try to execute itself. Consciousness permanently wants to get rid of consciousness, but it cannot.

Q: So, this experience of burning will never stop?

K: Why should it stop? For who? You still hope that when you're burnt out then there's a body that's burnt out and then you will be in peace? A nice idea!

Q: At least there will be less pain...

K: There will always be pain. Who needs less pain? That's what we're talking about. Less pain means you have a control system about your body. You find a way of accepting it and by accepting it, maybe it would be less painful. So even your acceptance is out of trying to control your pain. Your tolerance... everything that you try is to control your pain. And your pain is that you exist, from the beginning! The moment you exist, you have pain, a discomfort of existence... less pain, more pain, whatever you try is to have less pain. And that confirms the one who needs less pain. Then you pay attention to those techniques of yoga... or whatever... or understanding anything because you want to have less pain. Then you come to Arunachala asking to be burnt out because you want to have less pain. That's your tendency... less pain. It's not peace, just less pain, less whatever, fighting with yourself. 'If I don't risk myself then I have less pain'.

All these ideas... all what you try... is what? Longing for comfort... and the more you control the pain, the more you're depending on absence of pain to have comfort. It's amazing, what a trick! What a trap! Then people say, 'I'm in less pain so I'm more in peace because I have no interest... so now maybe I'm closer to peace'. I just point it out. 'Now I accept myself, now I love myself, now I have less pain'. Who needs that? Who needs less pain... that's the question? And who has pain now? Who needs any advantage anyway? Say it!

[Group]: 'Me'...

K: That's 'me'... always me, me, me! And what is there when 'me' is? More or less me-sery, and 'me'-stake... especially when *you're* at stake, that's the biggest mistake! You take yourself as the steak, that's the 'me'-steak... having a body and then fighting for some health in that body. A healthy me-steak. What to do? Try your best... but it will never be good enough. Then you have a burnt out body that dies... so, what? Your rainbow body was in harmony and then it dies in harmony, rest in peace.

Q [Another visitor]: How do I need to be executed?

K: You can only execute yourself by being That what doesn't know itself... being That what doesn't know what it is and what it is not. That is executing that false idea of yourself. The moment you know yourself, then it's already false. It's like an existence which is a depending existence. There's a dependency in it... and that you cannot accept. By that non-acceptance, you're longing for that what doesn't have to exist to exist. The moment you know yourself, you become a knower... then you have something to lose or to gain. There's a gainer and a loser... there's an ownership. The owner has more or less. The owner, having more or less peace is looking for peace, fighting for peace... because peace is what he's longing for. Whatever peace you can find is fake. It comes and goes. It's part of the coming, fleeting shadows of experiences. So, even in Samadhi, the peace you can experience is not the peace you are. It's not bad... when the mind is realizing, it's okay... but it's not good enough. It doesn't kill the mind, because there's still a mind to realize. There's a mind who understood, there's an understanding of the mind. That's okay... but it's not good enough for you because What you are is in *spite* of the mind understanding or not understanding... not because!

So the Peace you are doesn't depend on the mind who understands or not. The realization of mind is very nice and very fine in the world... but not for What you are. It's not good enough!

So, you have to see the emptiness of the realization of the mind. Whatever the mind is realizing is empty or false... it's as artificial as the mind is. It's temporary... it comes and goes. So, it's like a ghost realization.

Q: How...

K: There's no 'how' in it. It's not how do you do? This cannot be done!

Q: When my mind realizes and is scared... what should I do? Or is it already too late?

K: It's too late... just do your best, and see that it's not good enough. I'm not a teacher of how to control your mind in any way. To execute the mind... is being that what doesn't know any mind... what is and what is not mind. At that moment you are the mind that doesn't mind the mind!

Q: What I'm talking about is fear...

K: Yeah but fear is there only when you *have* a mind. When you *are* the mind, there's no fear. When you have a mind then you fear. When you have an existence, when there's ownership... then you fear. Fear is only there in the false evidence that you are. Fear means False Evidence Appearing Real. That appearance... that evidence that you have... this 'me', this mind that I can experience... is a *false* evidence, because it needs an evidence to exist. And whatever needs an evidence to exist, is false, because That what is the Absolute existence doesn't need to exist to exist. It doesn't need any proof of existence. The Truth you are never needs to be proven. It doesn't need any confirmation of any kind. And that what now has experiences is just a story. A story of the mind, of 'me' and all of that. It started at one point and at one point it will be over... but What you are... it was, it is and will be what it is... in spite of that story of the one that is, or is not, in peace.

These *samadhis*, this peace and things... whatever can be given... is a dependency. So, peace off. Because That what you are doesn't need any peace and that what needs peace will never find peace. For there's no peace in the world, there's no peace in anything because they are all ideas! The peace you are, you never lost. That what you never lost, you cannot find in any of this so-called... whatever you call it. The peace you can experience is not the peace you are... because the peace you can *experience* is different from something else. Sorry!... actually I'm not so sorry, I'm quite happy about it... if it goes that far.

Be happy that you don't have to be happy! And that happiness you are doesn't know any difference between that and That. That Absolute indifference of whatever is... cannot be achieved by any difference-making mind because the mind needs differences to survive. But what you are doesn't need anything. So what?

Then the mind even comes up with 'Oh, I'm the unborn. I'll take some landing in the unborn. I'm not born so I don't die'. It's trying to control fear again... because I'm not born, I don't fear. Who needs to be unborn not to fear? Osho's tombstone says 'Never born never died'... ha, ha, ha. 'I leave you my dream'... ha, ha, ha [Derisively]

Q [Another visitor]: What did he mean?

K: Don't ask me. [Pointing to a visitor] Ask her, she was with him. He was holding her hand when he died. Why should I talk about the bullshit what Osho said?

Q: That was a pretty dumb thing for him to say...

K: Why not? Maybe he was realized that he was Parabrahman and he was just leaving the dream for that what is in the dream, who knows? I can make it a good thing and I can make it a bad thing. Whatever you ask me. I can make him a Realized one because he was Parabrahman leaving the dream. But even that would be bullshit... because how can he leave his dream behind?

Q: I know...

K: I know! But I don't have to punish him all the time.

Q [Another visitor]: Several times you said you will kill me...

K: I killed you the moment I saw you, I don't have to kill you further! Because I never met you... by that I killed you already. So I cannot kill you further... there's no 'after' that. The moment I saw whatever this is is a shadow, I killed it... because it was not real! How can I kill a shadow? Do you think I have an interest to kill a shadow? What is in it for me? What do I get out of killing shadows? I have fun shooting ducks, that's all. [Laughter] And in a fair the ducks come back again and again. So I can kill them as much as I can and they are not dead. They are not even alive how can I kill them? So, don't have false hope here. Kill what can be killed and be that what is.

It has already happened, don't look at me. [Laughter] The moment you say hello, it's already 'Good bye!'

Q [Another visitor]: Am I the beast? [Laughter]

K: Some would agree. [Laughter] If you ask me like that I would agree... yes you are the beast. When God knows himself as 'someone', he becomes a beast, you know that: it's already the beast. Does it have any consequence if it experiences itself as a beast? That what is the Absolute experiencing itself as the be-east here and now?

Q: But there is...

K: There's nothing else... now you experience yourself as a beast but does it make you a beast?

Q: No...

K: So what is your question then? Just have fun with your beast.

Q : It's scary sometimes...

K: For who? Just be the beast. The beast cannot be scared by the beast, come on! Now you make a second beast... 'I'm scared about my own beast. I'm scared about what I can do to anyone'. I think everyone is scared about what he could do if the circumstance would be in whatever way, then the beast may wake up. Then you do things you never dreamt about. You take yourself as quite peaceful and something... 'I would never kill anyone. I cannot kill a fly on the wall, not me'. And then suddenly the beast comes up. [Laughter]

This helplessness I talk about... it's totally unpredictable! The circumstance dictates how you are in that particular moment... it's not in anyone's hands. It's the same with understanding: the understanding happens if the circumstance allows it. But not anyone who allows the circumstance to be. So, what to do? Already you are totally fucked! [Laughter]

Q: I don't know. Can you tell me?

K: Who gave me this job? [Joking] What have I done for this destiny? I have to listen to these questions. We can have the questions from the other side, this side is totally fucked up.

Q [Another visitor]: When do we know we are unfucked?

K: If you don't know anymore if you are the fucker, the fucking and the fucked... then you're unfucked! Then there's fucking, but without the fucker... then you are unfucked because you didn't exist because of fucking. Now you imagine that because of the fun of your parents you became a fun-tom – a phantom fuck creating a phantom person, a phantom fucker. Then this phantom fucker fucking again with another phantom fucker and creating another phantom fucker. That's the story of all fun fuckers.

The laziness is when you cannot get it up anymore, never got it up anyway... then you're really unfucked! But then you're fact, because you're not existing because of fucking. Then you're a fact but not a fucker! A fucker needs to know where he comes from and who is fucking and what is fucking. The Absolute unfucked is what you are... that is fact! It is satis*fact*ion not satis*fuck*tion... otherwise everything is a mind fuck. So, be the Absolute fucker who never fucked anyone, especially not himself, because there are no two. Because for fucking it needs two... and fucking is a mind fuck because separation is only in the mind. The mind fucks itself all the time creating another mind... me, myself and I fuck. Being

What you are... there's no such thing as me, myself and I. That's why it's called Silence.

But by all the fucking you do in the mind, you cannot become the unfucked. Whatever you try by fucking, you create another fucker who survives by fucking.

Q [Another visitor]: So, let the fucking happen and enjoy the show?

K: Even that is fucking... by trying not to fuck in the fucking you just become a quiet fucker. It doesn't work. Temporarily you get out of it... but only temporarily, because in one moment you can be interested again in fucking, then you fuck again. For a while you don't fuck. It's like a seeker who gave up seeking is still a seeker. He called off the search, but there's still a seeker who is not seeking. Then there will be some interest coming again out of the blue... and then he seeks again. For a while... maybe by understanding, or by so-called relative peace, the seeking stops by itself... and then out of the blue it starts again.

The little consciousness of the seeker tries to expand into the cosmic consciousness and maybe by whatever you have done you even achieve that. From the relative finite you become the infinite. You come from the finite to the infinite, from the *jiva* to the Shiva... from the little comic strip consciousness to the cosmic consciousness. That's quite nice, I don't deny that, but when you are That again, you forgot all what happened in this little one... and then you jump again in the next little one. Then you have to experience it again! There's no way out.

The cosmic one is the absence of separation, and the comic one is the presence of separation... that's the presence and the absence. But what you are is neither presence nor absence. These are the two faces of Shiva... experiencing himself as *jiva* or as Shiva. Like tonight is full moon, total *jiva* and in two weeks in no-moon during Shivaratri, it is Shiva *shambhu*, the Unconditioned one. The moon and the no-moon. There's a *jiva* in the moon, that's rising now to the full expansion of the ego. Then it goes back to the no-moon...

to no ego... from the 'me' to the no 'me'. These are the two main ways of realizing yourself, in a relative way and a non-relative way, in the absence and the presence. But what you are is neither present in the presence nor absent in the absence. You are always That. This is the basis of *neti-neti*.

So you're not present in the presence and you're not absent in the absence. By not knowing what you are and what you are not, you are neither present in the presence or absent in the absence. That is What you are... but you will never know *what* That is... you can never define That. This is the main definition: the presence is the definition and the absence is the definition, but That what is *defining* itself... in presence and absence, can never be defined! But in the presence there's an experience of a relative definer defining itself, and in absence not...but both is defining itself from that Absolute definer. But by all that definition, it cannot be finer. So you are not finer in the presence or in the absence. The Absolute definer doesn't get more in the presence or less in the absence. You are That what is imagining everything but cannot imagine Itself... and you cannot get bigger in presence or smaller in the absence. You are absolutely independent in any way you experience yourself. You are unconditioned by whatever... so none of what you can experience can condition That what you are. So, what to do?

But now you try to become That... and that is the joke. I'm talking to That what was never conditioned by whatever. Having a body doesn't make you a body. The body experience doesn't make you a body, the mind experience doesn't make you a mind, the absence doesn't make you the absence. You are always in *spite*... and never changed by anything. There's change and there's no-change... but if you would depend on no-change, you would still depend on no-change. So you are *not* changed by the change and not changed by the not change – neither-neither. So, what to do?

And That is what you cannot *not* be... so just *be* That. Be that laziness. Presence... aha! Absence... aha! Aha, aha, aha! Da, da, da... [Laughter] And that is always... always. Always uninterrupted what it is... not even interrupted by presence or absence! And that you cannot wrap in anything, you cannot take home... and that doesn't need to be understood because understanding is in presence, but whatever is in the presence, you leave in the absence. In the absence there's not even one who understood or didn't understand. There's neither a knower or what can be known... but still you are!

So what is in for you in the presence of understanding? Enjoy it... but it cannot give you anything! It doesn't make you more or less as you are... as the absence doesn't make you more or less as you are. There will always be presence and absence... and whatever is in the presence will be gone again... so whatever comes, is already gone. So, it's like a cemetery experience. The cemetery experience cannot kill you and this other cemetery experience... the absence which is like the experience of death, cannot make you less and experience of life cannot make you Life. You are That what you call Life in spite of experiencing life or no-life. That is Eternal Life and not what you can experience as life.

So, I don't deny all of this... this is just one side of your realization. But you cannot get unreal here or more real there. For the unreal doesn't make you unreal and the so-called real doesn't make you real. You are beyond in that way, beyond... of real and unreal... of good and bad... of day and night... of light and darkness. But they are all there because you are... but you are not because that is. And I can only point to that, I can only talk to That. I can only talk through these belief systems to that what doesn't need to believe anything... because that what is the be-leave system left in that way: it left that what is not a belief, that what doesn't need to believe in itself. But now you have a belief system, like a religion, and you now try to get out of it. But whatever you try to get out of the presence, puts you in the presence. What a joke!

In that sense I don't try to make anyone understand anything. And if it happens, it was not meant. [Laughter]

Q [Another visitor]: So even wanting to listen to you is just another trap. Just postponing?

K: She doesn't want to be here. She looks for a reason to be here and then she says, Oh it's not my fault. I don't want to be here but I have to be here. Trying to justify what never needs to be justified. Trying to find a base, trying to find a ground for why things are here.

Be That what is realizing itself and doesn't need any reason. There's no 'why' in it. For what you are, there's just 'why not'? Why not? Does it make you more or less? Does anything happen for what you are? Does anything make you more or less as That what you are? There's no trap for you. Even to say this is a trap is a trap. But there is no trap. You are untrappable. But you try to trap yourself because you think you are a mouse... and you're looking for a cat to eat you. That's fun.

Q [Another visitor]: So where did he go? [Laughter]

K: Osho never existed.

Q: But he said I leave you my dream...

K: You would say some other bullshit when you die. Do you exist? As much Osho existed, you exist. Why talk about the dead anyway? That's why I'm not interested in this person, you know that. I'm not interested in a tombstone coming from Australia. [Laughter] Once there was Osho and now there's no show. The only way I kill him is by saying 'Oh as Osho I was not so bad either'. Then he's dead. But I like to make him alive and put some fire under his arse, especially for the Osho widows who believe that they had a guru once and still hanging on ... 'Oh my Osho, my Osho'.

Q [Another visitor]: Do you know your horoscope is on the internet?

K: I know but why should I care? It's a horror scope. The moment you are born you have a horror scope. Then they give you a name and you have a sick nature because you have a signature. Then you are signed into doing that bullshit. Then you have a mother and father, then you're really fucked! And now you want to get out of it... but as much as you want to get out of it, you are in it.

The Germans they went to Poona and burnt down their bloody passports and said 'Now I'm not a German anymore'. They all got a new name... 'Now my name is Shiva'. From one bullshit to another bullshit! Then everyone is proud about their new names. They think now I left my name and now I'm in the cosmic and now I'm Shanti, Shanti, tra... la... la... [Laughter]

It's amazing! What bullshit one tries to get rid of oneself. Trying every different name. No one wants my names! [Laughter]

Q [Another visitor]: You don't give them...

K: Some people asked and I gave a name but no one wanted them. [Laughter] In German it is *Ma hat ma -Ma hat ma nich*. [Laughter] It means sometimes you have and sometimes you haven't. Or *gurnz-dursch-einander* [Laughter] There's Ananda that's totally mixed up. Or *nich all beieinander* – not all together. No one wants that. [Laughter]

But that's fun. Imagine you go in Germany and someone asks you what's your name? *Nich all beieinander*. [Laugher] That brings joy to people and not Shanti Devi or something. All these big names. Hanumans... [Yawning] I was driving *Hanumangarh* in Germany. It's a name for a tractor. And everyone thinks my name is now strong – Shiva or Parvati or Pragati.

Q [Another visitor]: Why does overloading happen so quickly? Sometimes you talk to one person and you get overloaded by that person...

K: Okay, try harder! Then you have to explode. Or you better implode... because it doesn't make such a big mess. You can implode now. Reduce yourself to that what you are... that's imploding... reducing yourself to That what cannot be reduced anymore. The substratum – that's imploding into the substratum. Just be the substratum which can never be reduced any further.

Q: What you are talking goes above my head...

K: I'm never interested in the head, you know that. Why should I talk to your head? That's imploding, abstracting everything what can be abstracted... but that what you are is the abstract itself, which cannot be further abstracted. That's imploding into That what you cannot *not* be.

Q: But it happens so quickly that you feel like... argh...

K: Good. Then it becomes so heavy it's unbearable... and I'm here to put more on it. I'm not here to make it lighter. I have to make it an unbearable lightness of existence because you try to bear existence, that's your problem. That's what makes you tired, trying to carry something what you cannot carry. It doesn't need to be carried... you're that what is unbearable, come on! And you try to bear that what is unbearable – yourself! Then you're tired...

Q [Another visitor]: When you speak of that Absolute longing, like being ten feet under water...

K: What you call the total longing can only stop by being What you are.

Q: It seems that at that point there must be such an unbearableness of even 'I Am'... and I can't create that ... I can't do anything about that. I can listen to you endlessly and sense that unbearableness but I'm not in that place yet of complete unbearableness of that 'I Am'. So what to do?

K: You can only surrender to that.

Q: But I can't even surrender...

K: It doesn't make a difference but maybe it makes it more bearable if you ask me.

Q: It's not in my hands?

K: No.

Q: How do I surrender?

K: Just surrender the surrendering... just accept that you cannot accept, surrender that you surrender. This comes from Ramana, surrendering of surrendering. It can not be done, it's just being what you are. Be as Absolute as you are... and there is no need for surrendering.

Q: I cannot even be as I am...

K: You cannot *not* be that Absolute you are... so be it! I can only repeat what he says – be as you are.

Q: But it has to be a hundred percent...

K: Hundred percent is not enough and zero is already too much. It doesn't need anything, that's the problem. You are here and now in spite. I can only make you attracted to That where I speak from and by that attraction alone you burn down.

Q: That's why I am here...

K: For that everyone is coming here... I want to make you an absolute addict for That what you are and by that addiction alone, by that surrendering to that addiction and your longing is being devoted only to That. This is like giving attention to only That what is what you are. That's burning you down... but not by trying to make it more bearable. So I try to make it something what is the only thing worth being... and the rest is... whatever it is. Who cares? Only being That what you are is ending all the beginnings.

Q: I feel the attraction to That as you speak. Your presence feels like a petrol to this fire. It is good to be in the presence of a Sadguru...

K: I would rather call it pre-sense and not the presence... that what is un-sensable, what is not part of the scenery. The pre-sense talking and the pre-sense listening are not different in nature. The pre-sense which is prior to all what can be sensed... the Absolute seer... the Absolute experiencer which is not an experience. From that certainty of being That, talking to That what is certainty there and not taking any bullshit anymore. Not taking *anything* anymore, not even *not* taking.

That is maybe creating a reference point which is not a reference point – a reference point where no one can be. That's all, because that kills. And every other reference point is just shifting between different positions and standpoints. But That has no standpoint. That never needs an anchor. It doesn't need any certainty, it *is* certainty. It is That and it's unshakeable by anything... and that cannot be transmitted. But you can talk to it. And by talking to it, in a way it gets activated in a way, that's all... if you are lucky, if it's meant to happen. But not by creating some harmony or peace or anything. It's absolutely independent of any agreement or if someone is pleased or pampered by it or feels good or bad. It's absolutely irrelevant.

So, by not trying to pamper anyone... this carelessness alone which is your nature, this reference point, or this helplessness or selflessness, call it whatever, you never left that. It is here now what you are and absolutely independent of all your imaginary dreams of existence or not. What else can I do? And not trying to please anyone, because what you are doesn't need to be pleased. So if I would try to please you, I would not honor you. I honor you only by not trying to please you – not at all.

Q [Another visitor]: When I listen to you, a fear arises. Is it the mind?

K: Whatever you believe it to be, you better fear me. I'm not here to make you more comfortable. It is meant to be killing what can be killed. That's why when Buddha met this assassin who had killed a thousand people... when the killer saw Buddha he bowed down to him and said 'You have killed much more than I ever can kill... by just looking at me!'

So just by being What you are, you kill the whole Universe, in one instant. So, I'm talking to That. Kill whatever can be killed... and be that what never needs to survive in anything. I'm not here to make survivors. And I'm not here to talk to tombstones. I'm not interested in walking tombstones who have some understanding... totally no interest!

Q [Another visitor]: There's a strong resonance to this ultimate freedom...

K: Now you define it again. Don't call it anything.

Q: We all want a Krishna, we all want to be a *gopi*...

K: You have to go to the toilet? She wants to go pee. [Laughter] Krishna was a cowboy like me.

Q: That's the problem, we are all *gopis* here trying to ask our Krishna how to...

K: How to ride the bull.

Q: I am more and more attracted now to this feeling of no more *gopi* or Krishna or whatever...

K: Yeah. Go and pee. [Laughter] You are the Absolute bladder and you have to pee anyway.

Q: And the final word I take from you is in spite...

K: ... spit on everything, even on the spitter, that's being in spite.

Q: So, no more Krishna, no more *gopi*...

K: Why not? It's fun. When you're Krishna, you're Krishna, when you're a *gopi*, you're a *gopi*, who cares? When you're French, you're French. So what? It's the worst case scenario I agree, but... [Laughter]

Q: You came into my life just to tell me that. And I thank you for that...

K: Aww... [Laughter] It's really like now it's okay to be French.

Q: I love you for that...

K: Today there was a guy in the Ashram who was blissed out and wanted to talk to me. I said, no no, *c'est la vie*!... No, I want to have questions, don't try to please me.

Q: No. I just try to please me...

K: It's strange. I can easily deal with offences, no problem. I cannot take love. Fuck off!

Q [Another visitor]: Do you think that giving you love is an offence?

K: Yes... the biggest offence, because you want to make me more as I am. You think you have love, that's really an offence. Whatever you try to give me is an offence – whatever! But especially love. [Laughter]

[A visitor cries]

They're all in Vrindavan... *rinderwahn* in German means mad cow disease.

Q [Another visitor]: It feels like being in a bottomless pit...

K: Is there any pit which has a bottom?

Q: I'm wondering if it's fear of losing control or the fear of absence...

K: Why should I know? Do you think I have an interest to know why you're fearing? Am I an oracle here? What is my interest to know why you fear? Because you exist, that's why you fear. The moment you exist, you fear... what else can you do? Existence is another word for existential crisis. That's the nature of existence – fear. Why thinking that I fear this pit? You fear even to exist. That's the basis of all, this existing 'I' – that is fear.

Q: Is there fear in existence and in non-existence?

K: You fear that you exist and that you even exist in non-existence... that you cannot get rid of 'you', that you fear most.

Q: So, I want to exist but I fear to exist?

K: You fear anyway. The moment you know yourself as existence, there's fear.

Q: The moment I know myself as non-existence?

K: You fear.

Q: Also?

K: Yes. Any knowledge is fear. Any knower who knows whatever he can know is fear. It comes with the knower, the moment 'you' exist or 'you' don't exist. Because you have to exist even to not exist so even that non-existence is fear. What to do?

So you have to be in spite of that what you are because the fear you cannot end. That's the way you realize yourself – fear: False Evidence Appearing Real. You cannot otherwise realize yourself in falsity... the false realizer being or not being. To be or not to be is the question of that one only. So, you have to be before that and during that and beyond that, whatever this is. But that's the way you realize yourself as one who exists or doesn't exist, in the presence and absence of that one. So, what to do?

If I sit here and tell you it will never stop, maybe you stop having interest in it, that's all. Because you are only interested because you hope that maybe one day you will control it, your fear. And if I tell you... fear will never stop... it never started and it will never stop, maybe your interest drops. And when there's no interest, who cares? Then there's peace... but not by you finding a way out of this or trying to stop the fear by understanding something. Whatever you try is controlling fear, out of fear. There's no end to it, finding a solution or anything... all of that is fake.

It's like a trick. If you see it will never stop, whatever you have done or not done, you will always fail to end fear... the interest drops, that's all. Then you will be surprised because for What you are there's no possibility of fearing anything. It's an imaginary... whatever. And you have an interest in an imaginary life... and this imaginary life is fear... and doubtful. Then there's permanent existential crisis. Then you cry for yourself, you're in a pity for yourself. [*Pretends to cry*] And all this poor me comes out of that false evidence or the false experience of the false existence.

You cannot put Reality in the unreal. The unreal will always be unreal and the fear is as unreal as that one who has fear. And it will never end... because the unreal will never become real, so what? Then you rest in That what doesn't need to be real, and has no idea about real or unreal. It was always there. But only your interest tries to make the unreal as real or tries to fix something which is unfixable. Even if you could fix it, you would fix an imaginary problem. What would be the advantage if you fix an imaginary problem? Then there's a fixed problem which is still imaginary. What is in it for you? Come on!

You are unfixable... and you always have to experience yourself as something that is unfixable. But experiencing yourself as someone who's unfixable doesn't *make* you unfixable... because what you are is beyond and prior to all of that... problem or no problem, or fixing and not fixing. Otherwise you always fix, fix, fix. You're trying to have hero-in and more-fine and maria-juana and you try to escape in understanding... oh God, oh God!

You show me whatever you have achieved and whatever you have learnt and I show you the emptiness in it. By none of that you can control anything. And by just being what you are you control the whole existence by being it. But the consequence of it is that you have no control about anything because there's no second existence. When you are that Absolute control, there is no controller... there's no two. But when there's two, there's one helpless controller trying to help another helpless controller.

So Being That what you are, the absolute consequence is that nothing has a consequence. All what you do or don't do has no consequence. There's no doership in anything... Absolute non-doership. And the main thing is that when you are that Life which is without a second life, there is no control possible – never was, never will be! There's not even freedom... you can never be free from yourself, come on! There's no freedom! From what? Another idea only. *Moksha*... have a mocha somewhere... that's enough *moksha*. You're being mocked by the idea of *moksha* and it's mugging you all the time by giving you a false idea of freedom... giving the false idea that you can leave this what you are. Mama mia...

You are That what is realizing itself as this, so what? And there's no beginning and no end in anything, this is the Eternal Life here now... and you are That. There's nothing you can do or not do.

And That is always realized because that is Reality realizing itself and nothing needs to be added to it. It will never be more or less as That. This is rest, this is what you are. This is rest... but you cannot rest in it because there's no one who can rest in that rest. But the moment you want to rest in that, you make it rest-less. The moment you want to make it *your* rest, you become restless. The moment you want to make it *your* home, you are homeless. So, what to do?

Q [Another visitor]: The beingness ends the suffering...

K: Suffering can not be ended. The problem is if someone tells you that I ended suffering, then he makes it real. If suffering really could end, it would exist. If seeking really existed and someone could end seeking, then seeking was real. What an idea! What a claim! It's amazing. If one claims that he realized his a true nature, then there's true nature. Fuck it!

Can I destroy something else? [Laughter]

Q: Is there no concept like pure beingness?

K: Fuck the pure and be what you are! You don't need to be pure... and that what needs to be pure is a false identity. Purity... what a dirty idea! [Laughter] It's the dirtiest idea you can have, the idea of purity. The biggest prison is the idea of freedom... you know that.

Q: I mean...

K: What do you mean? You become mean to yourself because you have a meaning. There's a 'me' who has a meaning. What is your meaning? What do you mean? [Laughing] Come on! [Silence]

Anyone else who has a meaning?

Q [Another visitor]: Why is there a tendency to go to places where saints or *avatars* live? Is it some kind of avoidance?

K: By instinct you go to a place where you maybe get killed... and you want to kill yourself, you know that. You are fed up with yourself. Everyone who comes to these places is fed up with himself... he wants to kill himself. This killer instinct, it brings you to places like that... 'Maybe there's a place that helps me to kill myself'. And you never know, so you go to these places for a little help. Maybe you get some extra energy from that place to kill yourself. Everything is possible.

You are already That what knows best what needs to happen. Who am I to decide? And if you decide by your instinct, the inner *guru* you are knows Absolutely why. You don't have to know why, It already knows why. Trust yourself totally... have faith in that guru you are. And that guru alone can kill the fake guru you believe in. Don't trust anything else as (much as) that guru you are.

I'm not here to make any disciples, I tell you. I try to kick them all off anyway. If I'm here, the Absolute intention is by talking to the guru you *are*... to make you the guru you are... and not the false guru you believe in. So, have total faith in That what you are and devote yourself only to that guru you are and not to anything that could be talked by your girlfriend or boyfriend.

Q [Another visitor]: Or you...

K: Did I give any advice what *you* should do? You should obey your boyfriend, that would be your peace. [Laughter] Can you handle that? No.

Q: I tried but I gave up...

K: That's the way of failing. [Laughing] It's in the Bible, you should obey your father, your mother and your husband and then you will be in peace.

Q: But if there's no-one... what can you do?

K: Who is this no-one you always talk about?

Q: Yeah. Forget it...

K: Yeah, forget the one and forget the no-one. Always these neo-advaita people reading one book and then giving satsangs. There's no one, who is asking this question? [Yawning] Kindergarden. I like Nisargadatta. He said this is not a kindergarden... this is for killing here and not for pre-schooling. This is after-school party. [Pointing to a visitor] You were there...

Q [Another visitor]: I was twenty seven and I didn't know much...

K: That is a good timing, Saturn return. [Laughter] So you are Sat yourself and you know the good timing to go to that place. In Saturn return it's really like a decision is taken... either you get married or you go for spiritual seeking. If you ask to many of the Osho guys when did you go to India, they'd say around twenty eight. It's always amazing... always in that time, there's a crucial point. If you have kids and things, and established in family you can continue. But if not, you have to go and look for something else. So, who can decide that until then?

Q: I asked him many silly questions that were coming from the mind and he sent me away. He said you go and meditate and come back... then you can ask questions... [Laughter]

K: I try the same but it doesn't work here.

Q: I went to thirty days of Vipasanna. Then I had a very deep zero experience in his presence. And then when I opened my eyes he said 'You need to ask from there'. And now here I am... [Laughter]

K: But that is proving my point. It doesn't have to stop, it will not stop. You can have the deepest of the deepest experience and it won't make any difference. But that's the best. Enjoy that it has no consequence for being what you are. There is no consequence... the dream continues. The next whatever is the next. The next sip of coffee or the next looking for... whatever... will be the next. And then, and then, and then, and then... Then there's no-then and even no-then is then... The absence is then... and then and then and then...

How to escape oneself? Impossible! So even the deepest of the deepest of the deep deep deepest experience of nothingness and zero zero, doesn't stop anything. Fantastic! What else I am always pointing to? In spite of being in spite, I have to sit in front of myself and talk to myself. What can I do? And that never started and will

PEACE OFF: AND BE WHAT YOU ARE

never stop. So, the moment I wake up, I talk to myself. Even in the absence, you start talking to yourself. There's a little discussion happening with yourself... [Laughter] 'How was my sleep? What happened? What is meant to happen today? Did I do something yesterday?' You always recollect your little self so that you can function. You start talking to yourself and loving yourself and caring about yourself... what can you do?

Q: Then there was years of meditation. When the peace got good enough, the unbearableness was not big enough. All of that was there and still... it's not unbearable enough...

K: It will never be unbearable enough, I tell you. You are always the Absolute who has no problem bearing itself infinitely. Now even the hope that one day it will be unbearable enough is fake. [Laughter] Who do you think you are? Do you think you are some little coolie bearing something that's loaded over him? No. You are the Absolute who has no problem bearing itself. There's no limit of what you can take because you *are* That and there's not even an effort of taking Yourself and bearing yourself.

So, even that idea or hope that one day it will be unbearable will not happen. Even the unbearable is bearable for what you are. Then the next starts... call it idea or not, it's like you realize yourself in lies, what can you do? It's called real-lie-zation. Lie by lie, moment by moment you lie to yourself. You are the liar, the lying and what can lie. What else can you do? You are the experiencer experiencing what can be experienced, the seer seeing what can be seen. What else? You start with a lie. The moment you exist, it's a lie... and that makes you a liar. And out of a liar comes lying... Brahma, the liar, the creator God. Then he lies to people by saying that he found the end of the light of Shiva. So you experience yourself as a liar, what can you do? But does it make you a liar? By experiencing yourself as a liar, you don't become a liar.

Q [Another visitor]: Are you sure?

K: Are you sure? What a question! Prove it to me? Is that faith?

Then it starts again... if there would be any, she would just listen and be quiet. But still there's doubt... and the doubt will never stop. You will always doubt what you say because you know it's not true. Every experience you doubt... and I tell you, be happy that you doubt it. You are right to doubt it. What to do?

I like that the certainty cannot be transmitted. You have to be what you are for yourself and no one can give it to you. There is no transmission... No way. And who cares if I am... whatever... you should only care if you are That. Even if I could prove what I say, why should you care if someone can prove anything? Who needs to be confirmed and who needs a confirmation and who would I be if I get a confirmation of someone who confirms me? What does it make me?

What you are never needs any con-firm-ation... it is that what is firm by itself. It cannot get more firm. That what needs confirmation by more understanding is... what? A never-ending story of... it's called a his-story... the story of Consciousness... which is already a doubtful existence. Always trying to make it un-doubtful... and never succeeds. Nisargadatta said, this Consciousness is unneeded and unwanted, you simply cannot get rid of it. So let it have its story. Let it play its game. But there's nothing in it for you... there was never anything in it for you in the first place. And it cannot give you anything and it cannot take anything from you. But you cannot get rid of it – that's all. Because already consciousness is a phantom experience. So what to do? You simply cannot get rid of it – that's all. But it cannot give you anything and it cannot take anything away.

But you're trying to fix consciousness – come on! And depending on consciousness who is in peace with itself and depending on consciousness who knows itself... that will never happen. Because if consciousness could know consciousness, there would be two consciousnesses. Already that is an idea. There's not even one consciousness! But then... imagining that consciousness has to realize consciousness... that makes it again two consciousnesses.

Out of one consciousness, it becomes two again.

That's what Happy-Nappy was saying... When there's oneness, there's twoness... because both come together. And only in consciousness there's oneness and twoness but not in what you are. So, what to do? I can only point to the false because you can never point out what is not false.

Q [Another visitor]: I have been quite emotional since I started coming to this talk and it has been quite intense. What to do?

K: That shows your helplessness... that you cannot get rid of emotions. As much as one tries not to have emotions because emotions hurt, you cannot get rid of it. They come. Tears come, emotions come – unexpected. Suddenly it runs... suddenly that whatever was held back just opens up because the controller is absent. It's just uncontrollable. You live yourself in all possibilities, in emotions and things... there's no right and wrong in it. But it's not out of pity, that's the main thing. It's not a self-pity emotion.

Q: No, there's no self-pity...

K: And that's the little difference. Normally one is crying out of pity then and tear jerking happens. [Laughter] You try very hard to be sad enough to cry. But this is not out of sadness or joy. Both are not there.

Q: What you say touches me in such a way that is unexplainable...

K: That is called compassion. When compassion touches... then, no way... you cannot hold. And then it runs, the whole energetic storage comes out... and maybe it's not pleasant sometimes. But that's the way it is.

[A visitor crying and panting]

Q [Another visitor]: This is like a train coming into a station... [Laughter]

K: You laugh... but you are the worst case scenario, I tell you! She cries like hell! It's a point of no return and then you really fear.

This heart quake is unbearable... it's a touch from your very core. The core is touched by the core... there's not an opening at all. It's like the dam is broken in a way... you are not damned anymore by ideas. The dam is broken and the emotions come as they come.

Q [Another visitor]: You said the core is touched by the core. That touched me... [Laughter]

K: And that is called compassion, because you're touched by your very Self and it is not something what you can avoid. It's the helplessness of being touched by What you are... no armour can ever stop that... being touched by What one is. When I say I talk to That what you are, you cannot avoid being touched because you cannot build an armour around it, because I talk from that where you already are and there's no defense system you can build up by any mind stuff or any armour or defence for that. Because I don't even have to penetrate anything to be you. This is an Absolute sex. [Laughter]

They say if the sword is sharp enough, it cuts without cutting... just by being the sharpness itself.

Q [Another visitor]: It sounds to me that what you're saying is to live the life that you are...

K: You are Life living life... Reality realizing Reality.

Q: And where are you in relation to that?

K: There's no 'me' in it. I have no idea what I am and what I am not.

Q: So Life is living itself?

K: Life is living life – that's all. But Life is not knowing what is life and what is not life. There's an absolute not knowing what is life and what is not life... that's the nature of life... and that's your natural state. But the moment you know what is life and what is not life... like life and death, then you're dead. That is dead knowledge.

The Knowledge is Knowledge not knowing what is knowledge and not knowledge.

Q: Is there a perception of Life living itself?

K: No. Life is living itself as a perceiver perceiving what is perceived... but not as Life. So, That what is the Father, what is the Spirit and what is the son is not different... it's only Heart. The Heart of the Father, the Heart of Spirit and the Heart of the Universe. You are That! That is Life living itself as the Father, living itself as the Spirit and living itself as the world. But it's not the way it's living itself... it's always That what is living itself and not knowing what it is and what it is not. So, you experience yourself as mind... but you are not mind. You experience yourself as father... but you are not the father or the son.

By not knowing what you are and what you are not, you are! You don't have to defend that, that's the beauty of it. That's the peace you are because that never needs to be defended. There's no defense system... no need for anything. That is satisfaction. But not by knowing yourself in anything. By not even knowing life – that's life!

Q [Another visitor]: But when you are talking, I perceive something in my heart and you're talking about Heart. So, can the Heart know?

K: Yes... it is knowledge.

Q: So that's why I could experience...

K: That's an Absolute experience of being Heart but without an experiencer: that's Heart because there is no ownership in that Heart. There's Heart without ownership. If I talk to that Heart which has no owner, than I'm talking to What I am... and then it's compassion. But not from one owner to the other. So I'm talking to the Absolute owner... which is Heart, the Kingdom of Heart and not to a king. I'm not interested in kings.

To be the kingdom is talking to the kingdom. But it's not trying to get another king learning how to control the kingdom. I'm not a teacher of control systems because Heart cannot be controlled.

But that is very emotional, which is Heart. This compassion has no limits. It is nowhere and everywhere... It's that what is. And you cannot *not* be touched by What you are... it's an Absolute touch by being it. That shows sometimes in the body as tears and emotions.... but you don't even know where it comes from. It's not triggered by something, it's just by being what you are. And this energy is unpredictable. What to do?

In that sense, I don't want to offend myself by giving anyone any teaching... because for me you are already That. That quality which is Quality. That treasure you are which you can only treasure by being it... and not by controlling it. There's no ownership in that treasure. The Peace which is what you are is the treasure. And treasuring your treasure is being That... but not knowing what it is. And the moment you want to know it, you are out of it. That's the whole problem. What to do?

Okay, that's the end of the season. I see you when I see you. [Laughter]

21th Feb 2016
Tiruvannamalai

www.ingramcontent.com/pod-product-compliance
Lightning Source LLC
Chambersburg PA
CBHW070645160426
43194CB00009B/1586